CYCLING FOR SPORT

MOUNTAIN BIKES, FREE RIDING AND SPORTIVE RACES

CYCLING FOR SPORT

MOUNTAIN BIKES, FREE RIDING AND SPORTIVE RACES

THE ULTIMATE VISUAL GUIDE TO MOVING UP A GEAR: THE CHALLENGES OF OFF-ROAD AND ON-ROAD CYCLING IN OVER 230 STEP-BY-STEP PHOTOGRAPHS

EDWARD PICKERING

southwater

This edition is published by Southwater, an imprint of Anness Publishing Ltd, Blaby Road, Wigston, Leicestershire LE18 4SE; info@anness.com

www.southwaterbooks.com; www.annesspublishing.com

If you like the images in this book and would like to investigate using them for publishing, promotions or advertising, please visit our website www.practicalpictures.com for more information.

Publisher: Joanna Lorenz
Project Editor: Anne Hildyard
Designer: Steve West
Jacket Design: Nigel Partridge
Production Controller: Bessie Bai

Previously published as part of a larger volume,
The Complete Practical Encyclopedia of Cycling

A CIP catalogue record for this book is available from the British Library.

ETHICAL TRADING POLICY
Because of our ongoing ecological investment programme, you, as our customer, can have the pleasure and reassurance of knowing that a tree is being cultivated on your behalf to naturally replace the materials used to make the book you are holding. For further information about this scheme, go to www.annesspublishing.com/trees

PUBLISHER'S NOTE:
Although the advice and information in this book are believed to be accurate and true at the time of going to press, neither the authors nor the publisher can accept any legal responsibility or liability for any errors or omissions that may be made nor for any inaccuracies nor for any loss, harm or injury that comes about from following instructions or advice in this book.

CONTENTS

Introduction

When you want to move your cycling progression up a gear, sportive events that take place in summer are the natural choice, or riding off-road on rough terrain. Although both types of cycling are open to all riders, a good level of fitness and training is essential.

Sportives, known as 'cyclo sportives', are long distance events in which the participants have to complete a course in a certain time limit. They are the equivalent of running a marathon in that the cyclists view them as a personal challenge in which they are not actually competing against other people. Both experienced racing cyclists and amateurs take part in sportives, although they can be extremely challenging and the riders need to be fit to take part.

Sportive events

Most are held annually and are generally between 100 and 200km in length. The long course usually has some particularly difficult parts, such as a series of climbs over the whole route or a steep uphill finish. One famous event, the Paris-Roubaix, is flat, but sections of the course are cobbled, so that the surface is bumpy, uncomfortable and difficult to ride on. Riders often modify their bike to lessen the shock of riding over such an uneven

Below: Riders face a steep and difficult uphill battle in a sportive event that includes a lot of climbing.

Above: When riding over muddy terrain, put the bike into low gear, and pick a line and stick to it. Keep your weight off the front wheel so you can pull it out.

surface. Thick tyres and strong wheels can help, and some riders tape the handlebars so that they can more easily grip them. There have been many injuries to riders and damage to bikes over the years in this race.

To succeed in these events, the style of bike and the materials it is made from are hugely important. The bike has to be light and fast, with narrow tyres and drop handlebars, with a frame that is less rigid than a racing bike, which makes for a more comfortable ride when cycling for long distances. Comfort is very important if you are to finish the course.

Frames made of carbon are popular because this material absorbs impact and is faster, but a good steel frame will last forever if looked after.

Mountain biking

Because this sport is usually off-road on rough terrain that may be muddy or rocky, a specialist all-terrain mountain bike is necessary for these conditions. Trail riding and cross country require certain skills, such as learning to absorb shocks on bumpy tracks and deal with muddy conditions and rocky paths, and learning to descend and climb safely.

A development of mountain biking is freeriding, which can involve jumping off mountains or over obstacles, or riding boards high off the ground in forests.

Other disciplines include four-cross, slalom, trials and dirt jump. At a four-cross event, four riders race elbow-to-elbow down a steep hill that has been laid out with corners and jumps at unpredictable places.

Slalom is an aggressive fight between two riders who are going head-to-head on two separate but almost identical courses downhill. The riders start separately but then their lanes merge, so each rider is desperate to gain supremacy by getting to the merged lanes first, since then he will have no difficulty keeping the lead to the end.

Trials entail following a course and jumping over obstacles without putting the feet on the ground, and no part of the bike except for the tyres can touch the obstacle. There is a time limit for completing the course and riders are penalized if they exceed it. This type of riding takes a lot of practice; skill and balance are required to balance on a rear wheel and hop on to an obstacle that is high in the air.

Dirt-jump is a spinoff of mountain biking, but it is not wholeheartedly recognized. Supporters of the sport build their own dirt-jumps, and claim that the sport is not about competition, rather that people perform tricks and jumps on the track in a way that best expresses their individuality.

The final section is all about getting fit, making sensible food choices and how to train effectively for endurance, speed and climbing.

This book will provide you with all the information you need to explore both on-road and off-road cycling, and rise to the challenge of mountain biking, freeriding and taking part in challenging sportive events.

Above: A mountain biker descends on a complex free-riding course, made from wooden logs.

Below: To negotiate a drop-off, the rider puts some weight over the back wheel and pulls up the handlebars. The back wheel will hit the edge and then go over.

SPORTIVES

Sportive rides are the perfect compromise between leisure riding and all-out racing. Sportives have elements of both, and the best thing about them is that you can choose how seriously, or not, to take the event. Sportives are billed as personal challenge rides. They usually take place over long, but not impossible distances, sometimes taking in famous climbs, or arduous terrain – they are challenge rides, after all. Many also offer shorter distance rides to complement the main event, which means they are more inclusive.

Above: A group of riders take part in a sportive ride.
Left: Sportive rides often take place in mountainous areas.

The Sportive Bicycle

A sportive bike can provide a similar performance to a racing bike. It is so similar, in fact, that most people who participate in both road races and sportives find that they can use the same bike without noticing any particular disadvantage.

Sportive bikes need to be reliable, light, fast, efficient and comfortable. They look very similar to racing bikes, with narrow slick tyres and drop handlebars. The only difference with a real high-end racing bike will be more relaxed geometry in the frame, which will make for a more comfortable ride over a long distance. A racing frame will be extremely rigid, so that little power is wasted in frame flex, while a sportive bike needn't be so rigid. However, in their speed and weight, they have far more in common with a racing bike than with a touring bike, for which comfort is everything.

Events

Sportives tend to range from 25km (15.5 miles) for a short distance event complementing another ride, to between 170 and 200km (105–125 miles) for the longest events. They often take a big loop into isolated terrain. It is important

Below: Sportive bikes need a good range of gears, and the compact chainset has become a popular choice because it offers the required flexibility.

Above: A typical sportive bike is lightweight so that riding up steep hills becomes easier, but it is also comfortable for riding long distances.

that the bike is well-maintained so it won't let you down at a critical time.

Although there are sportives in all regions, from flat to mountainous, many take place in the Alps and northern Italy, where the routes take in large climbs. Popular British sportives are also very hilly, so a lightweight bike could help to make the difference between a gold and silver award.

Go for comfort

The length of most sportive events means that comfort is important. While a stiff, lightweight racing bike is the fastest option, don't sacrifice comfort for speed. If you do, you will ride the first two hours faster, then slow down for the second half of the event, as the discomfort increases. All except specialized racing bikes are suitable for sportive events.

The debate about frame materials continues, and there is no simple answer. The best material for one person may not be the most suitable for another. If you can afford a carbon fibre or aluminium frame, these will get you round the course the fastest. These frames are unlikely to last for a lifetime, however, while a good quality steel frame will last forever, well maintained.

After choosing which frame to use, the next most important decision involves gearing.

Racing bikes are designed for high speed events, and come with 52–42 or 52–39 chainrings, and 12–21 or 12–23 blocks on the back. For flatter sportive events, these might be sufficient but it is worth considering getting a compact chainset, with 50–34 rings, for riding in the hills. For self-sufficiency, make sure you can carry two water bottles, a pump, and a saddlebag or panniers containing spare tubes and tools.

Right: Fit a saddlebag with spare inner tubes and tyre levers.

Anatomy of a sportive bike

❶ Wheels: Size 700 x 23C with 28 or 32 spokes to save weight, narrow-section rims for aerodynamics, slick tyres for lower rolling resistance.

❷ Frame: Can be steel, or more modern lightweight materials such as carbon fibre or aluminium. Geometry is less relaxed than a touring bike, and similar to that of a racing bike, for a faster, more responsive ride.

❸ Brakes: Lightweight good quality calliper brakes. Models such as the Campagnolo Chorus and Shimano

Ultegra are popular, with very good performance.

❹ Chainrings: Compact chainsets, with a smaller inner ring, are becoming very popular with sportive riders. Fifty teeth on the bigger ring and 34 on the smaller is a good combination. Or possibly a racing set, with 52–42 toothed rings. Some people put a triple chainring on their sportive bikes, especially in mountainous events.

❺ Sprockets: Ten-speed freewheel, with a 12–25 block. For very steep

and long hills, depending on the chainring size, it might be advisable to fit a 27-tooth sprocket.

❻ Gear changers: Combined with the brake levers to save weight and for accessibility while riding.

❼ Saddle: Comfortable but narrow.

❽ Handlebars: Drop handlebars offer a range of positions. Riders can be aerodynamic on descents, and sit up for ease of breathing on the climbs.

❾ Pedals: Lightweight clipless pedals for shoes to attach to directly.

Clothing for Sportives

Sportive riding is a summer sport, so clothing needs to be lightweight, breathable, comfortable and aerodynamic. Modern fabrics are perfect in that they keep the body cool if necessary and also can act as insulation in cold weather.

One of the most important items of clothing for summer riding is a pair of Lycra racing shorts with a synthetic padded insert. For long rides on a fairly hard and narrow saddle, comfort is paramount. Ordinary cycling shorts are fine, but many racers wear bib shorts, which have straps stretched over the shoulders. Bib shorts fit snugly, and can be a more comfortable option over long distances.

Cold conditions

On chilly days, it is also worth covering the knees to protect them from the cold – longer shorts are available, but a better solution is to get some detachable knee warmers that extend from the thigh, inside your shorts, down to below the knee. If it warms up, you have the advantage that you can take them off.

A base layer is a good idea, even on hot days. Base layer garments wick sweat away from your body. In mountainous events, it can get quite chilly when descending, especially at altitude, and if you are covered in sweat this can be a problem. The lightest base layers have plenty of ventilation – some are string-vest style, which help keep you cool on hot days.

Wear an ordinary cycling top over your base layer. This should not be too baggy, otherwise it will catch the wind and slow you down. On the other hand, don't squeeze into a top that is a size too small either – find a comfortable snug-fitting breathable cycling top.

Like knees, arms can get chilly on cool days or on long descents. If it looks like being a cold day in the saddle, wear some detachable arm warmers. These will add a crucial layer of insulation, and

Right: For a sportive, lightweight, breathable clothing will make the event more comfortable.

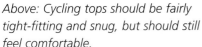

Above: Cycling tops should be fairly tight-fitting and snug, but should still feel comfortable.

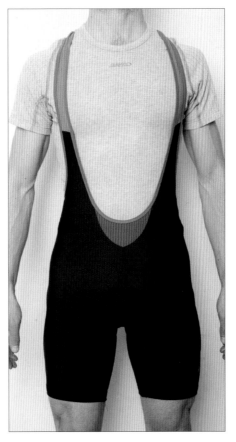

Above: Padded bib shorts over an insulating base layer are comfortable and aerodynamic.

Above: In cooler conditions, a gilet and arm warmers add an extra layer.

pack down compactly if the day warms up. On cool days, also consider a gilet, which is a sleeveless zip-up top to insulate the body.

Footwear

Shoes should be stiff-soled, with attachments for shoeplates, which clip into the pedals. The stiff soles ensure that your feet do not bend around the pedals and so stop you wasting energy, and stop the feet becoming sore. Your shoeplates should use the same system as your pedals. Most shoes can accommodate all the main industry standard systems. When choosing shoes for size, be aware that your feet expand in the heat, so if they are tight when you buy them, they will be tighter when you are some distance into an event. You don't need to buy excessively loose shoes, but do buy for comfort. Shoes with Velcro fastenings are the most popular: they are easy to put on and take off, and can be loosened temporarily if your feet get uncomfortable.

Headgear

Most sportive organizers insist that you wear a helmet. It should pass all the safety standards (as should all helmets sold). The helmet should fit snugly and not move when the head is shaken about, and should also be well ventilated. Replace your helmet every two years, and at once if it suffers an impact (even if no damage is visible).

Sportive wear
Cycling shoes: Stiff-soled for efficiency
Cycling socks: Insulated
Cycling bib shorts: Padded
Knee warmers: Optional, for cooler days
Base layer: To wick away sweat
Cycling top: Lightweight and breathable
Arm warmers: Optional, for cooler days
Gilet: Optional, for cooler days

Above: Road cycling shoes are stiff-soled for better power transmission, and fastened with Velcro.

Above: If you are going to wear a helmet for a few hours in hot weather, comfort and coolness are important.

Setting Goals

Before entering a long-distance sportive, it is sensible to attempt to achieve the necessary level of fitness first. If you are an experienced participant in other sports, your fitness should transfer easily to cycling.

Your sportive riding experience will be more positive if you use it as a long-term goal, with a sensible build-up and a commitment to do your best.

Before entering an event, you need to assess two things – current ability and potential ability. You can then set your long-term goal and, with that in mind, decide how much training you are going to need to do to fulfil your potential.

If you are starting from zero, with little exercise in the last few years, the first thing you need to do is go to see a doctor for a medical check. Once you have the all-clear to begin your exercise regime, build up slowly and get used to riding the bike and accustom yourself to the physical exertion. It is realistic to set a goal of entering a shorter sportive within a few months, but try to think in terms of using shorter events and the time between them as stepping stones to a longer event a year down the line.

Commit yourself
You will get the most out of yourself and the sport if you work on the principle of building up to a certain level, consolidating your fitness, then using that as a foundation upon which to build your step-up to the next level. In other words, make the bike into a lifestyle choice, and commit to

Above: Running provides good base fitness and lower-body workouts that are beneficial for cyclists.

improving yourself continuously. You will be amazed at how far you can make yourself go in this way. Over a few years, you could be riding 50km events in your first season, 100km events in your second, and full-length 170km sportives in your third. Along the way you will reduce body fat levels, become more toned, massively increase your energy levels, and achieve some incredible goals. If you are new to cycling, but are fit and have kept up an interest in other sports, it is realistic to set higher goals, but you must still be aware that it will take time for your body to adapt to the new stresses you are placing on it. With an adaptation period, and a sensible build-up, it is realistic to envisage riding a 100km event within three to six months of starting out, while

What should your goals be?

Cyclist
Achievements attainable for a racing cyclist:
In 3 months: full-length sportive, silver standard
In 6 months: full-length sportive, silver standard
In 1 year: full-length sportive, gold standard
Long-term goal: Finish in top 20 of a big sportive

Commuting leisure cyclist
In 3 months: 50km sportive
In 6 months: 100km sportive
In 1 year: full-length sportive
Long-term goal: silver standard in a long sportive

Non-cyclist
Achievements attainable for a regular sports player:
In 3 months: 100km sportive
In 6 months: full-length sportive
In 1 year: full-length sportive, silver standard
Long-term goal: gold standard in a full-length sportive

Sedentary individuals
In 3 months: 50km sportive
In 6 months: 50km sportive, at a faster pace
In 1 year: 100km sportive
Long-term goal: full-length sportive

Above: After an organized training build-up, you are ready to enter your first sportive.

keeping an eye on setting a longer term goal of a full-length sportive within a year.

If you have ridden your bike regularly as a commuter or leisure cyclist, the adaptation should be straightforward, since your body is used to spending time in the saddle. The challenging part will be twofold – you need to get used to riding long distances, and you also need to get used to riding a little faster. The

easiest adaptation comes from racing cyclists who want a less time-intensive and stressful goal than road racing. Most amateur racing events are under 100km, so it takes a little extra time to get used to the longer distances. If the body is already used to cycling training, just alter the workouts a little.

Of course, most people fall somewhere in between all these categories. They also react differently to training – some become fitter very quickly, others take time to adapt. Some enter a marathon event such as the Tour de France's Etape du Tour,

Above: Mountain bike enduro events are a good target for riders who are aiming to increase their fitness.

which is a 180km ride through some of the most challenging mountain roads in cycling, with only a few months to train. The important thing is to always be aware of the signals your body is sending out.

Below left: Swimming helps to achieve stamina, strength and suppleness.
Below: Athletes who play sports such as tennis will build fitness quickly.

What to Expect in a Sportive

There are hundreds, if not thousands, of sportive events organized around the world, and each one is different. Some are very flat, while others include multiple climbs of 30km (18 miles). Some start with 5,000 riders or more; others attract 100 competitors.

Although a good foundation of base fitness in cycling will help you to get round any sportive fairly easily, training needs to be geared to the specific event you have entered. Before entering, try to find out as much information about the route as you can. Most events have internet sites, with downloadable maps and profiles of all the routes.

The profile is the most important part. It will show all the climbs and descents. Sometimes the scale can be misleading, so check the altitude scale on the left-hand side of the profile. Most sportive events have one, two or three signature climbs, which will be the main challenges of the day, and your success will depend largely on how well you pace yourself on these climbs.

The ups and downs of racing

If an event includes a long climb, your training and preparation need to take this into account. A 15km (9 mile) climb places severe stresses on the body, and if your training rides all took place on flat roads, your body will be less able to deal with the challenge. Make sure that your training includes climbing. If you live in a flat area, consider going on a training camp in a hilly or mountainous area. If you have a good level of base fitness, a week spent in the mountains will allow your body to adapt to the rhythm and techniques of long climbs. Not all events take place in the high mountains; there may be many shorter climbs, of between 3 and 7km (2 and 4 miles) in length. None are very hard in themselves, but the repetition makes each subsequent climb harder than the last. These are easier to train for – just try and replicate the number and length of climbs in your long training rides.

The downhill and flat sections are just as important – look at the profile to see where they are. A long descent is a

Above: Hilly sportives will test your fitness to its limits – success in these events depends on your long-term training technique.

good time to recuperate, so it might be worth trying a little harder on the climb in the knowledge that you have plenty of time to recover from the effort. Alternatively, some climbs lead you on to a plateau, or to the base of another climb – you'll need to be aware of the shorter recuperation time involved.

Steep terrain

Profiles can be misleading. Organizers concentrate on including the major climbs, but they may just draw a flat line between them. In reality, these flat sections may be a series of rolling climbs, with steep sections that sap your strength. Be prepared for this eventuality.

Left: The Etape du Tour follows the same route as a mountainous stage of the Tour de France and attracts thousands of entrants.

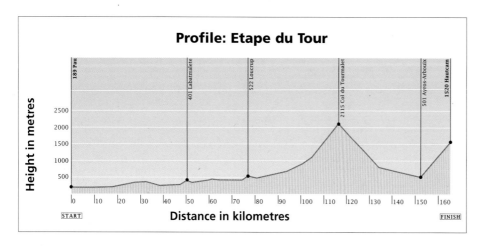

Profile: Etape du Tour

Height in metres: 2500, 2000, 1500, 1000, 500

189 Pau · 401 Labatmalete · 522 Loucrup · 2115 Col du Tourmalet · 501 Ayros-Arbouix · 1520 Hautcam

Distance in kilometres: 0, 10, 20, 30, 40, 50, 60, 70, 80, 90, 100, 110, 120, 130, 140, 150, 160

START · FINISH

On the day

Most events start in the morning, so, depending on how far you live from the ride, it might be better to arrive the day before.

When you arrive, set up your bike so it is ready for the event. Pump up the tyres, make sure the components are clean and working well, double-check that the saddle and handlebars are in the correct position, and test the gears and brakes.

If you have had a long drive, your legs will be a little stiff, so it's a good idea to test the bike out on a short and easy ride. This is not the time for training – just a 30-minute easy ride to get your bike and body ready for the next day. Bring a spare set of kit for this ride, so you don't get your event clothes dirty or sweaty. Sometimes it is possible to sign on the day before, and you should do this if possible, so you can get your race number on the bike and avoid queues on the morning of the event.

The evening before, wrap your food and pack it into your pockets, prepare your drinks, eat a large dinner and get a good night's sleep. On the morning of the event, get up in plenty of time to eat a reasonable breakfast and get to the start. In larger events you will be directed to a pen according to race number, but in all cases, the earlier you arrive, the closer to the front you will be. If you want to win the event and you start at the back, you'll have several hundreds or thousands of riders to pass. Help yourself by getting there in good time. You are now ready to go.

Above: Riding consistently well in a hilly sportive depends on fitness and determination – but the effort will be worth it.
Below: The Gran Fondo Pinarello is one of the biggest and most famous sportive events in Italy – its mountainous profile makes it a serious physical challenge.

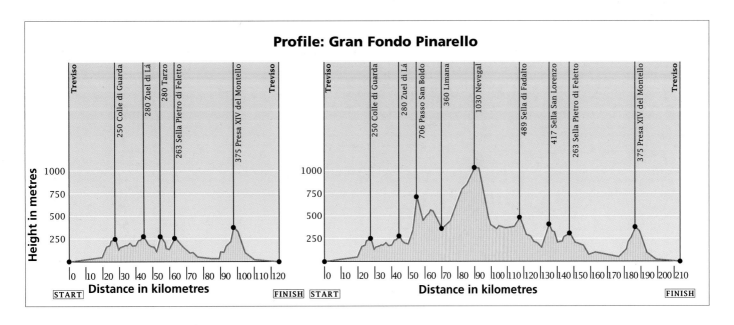

Pacing and Gearing in a Sportive

Riding a sportive is not about pedalling like fury as soon as the gun goes off. Strategy and tactics and a thorough awareness of your own capabilities are more likely to get you to the finishing line with the chance of a good result.

A sportive is a race, so you naturally want to get around the course as fast as you can. But this does not involve putting your head down and riding hard from the gun. By riding intelligently, spreading out your effort and concentrating on riding as efficiently as you are able, you will achieve the best possible result.

Pacing

To succeed at pacing, you must look at the profile, have an awareness of your own ability and knowledge of the conditions on the day and be flexible in case of surprises. Preparation helps here – set your bike up correctly, with the right gears, and train for the challenges of your specific event. The best way to maintain a pace you know you can handle is by using a pulse monitor during training and the event. The effort you are making when cycling is reflected in a higher pulse as your heart works harder to transport blood to the muscles. Training with a heart monitor is covered on page 155, but the main point to remember is that you can only sprint for a limited period, whereas a steady, controlled effort can be sustained for longer.

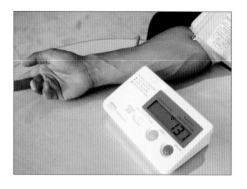

Above: A digital machine measures the pulse and blood pressure.
Below: Riding steadily over long distances will get you to the finish faster.

This is not a foolproof way of looking at it, since other factors, such as refuelling, previous efforts and even general tiredness also have a big effect on fatigue levels. However, by using a pulse monitor as a guide, you can maintain a sustainable level of effort. The more experience you gain in training and riding sportives, the more you will understand the way your body in particular reacts to the effort.

When no other factors are taken into consideration, it is theoretically ideal to maintain the same pulse rate and level of effort all the way through an event, but it is more realistic to anticipate changes of pace according to circumstances and the way you feel.

The golden rule, especially for inexperienced riders, is not to go too hard at any time. Accumulated fatigue can mount very badly if you go too hard early on. One good way of avoiding fatigue is to train yourself to spin the pedals faster in a lower gear. Different riders' bodies work efficiently at different pedalling rates, but according to sports doctors, pedalling a large gear slowly places greater stress on the muscles, which tire quickly, and pedalling a small gear fast places greater stress on the cardiovascular system while saving the muscles. Train yourself to turn the pedals at 90 revolutions per minute, and your body will become more efficient at handling the effort.

Gearing

For a mountainous sportive, it is a good idea to be conservative in your choice of gears. Fatigue builds up insidiously on long climbs, and if you are feeling weary, and already in your bottom gear, you can lose a lot of time.

Racing bikes tend to use 52 and 42 rings on the front, and 12–21 or 12–23 at the back. This is good for the fast and intense pace of a short race. However, for a sportive and for riders who are less fit, there is little point in trying to ride the same gears as a racer.

To provide lower gears, you can either fit larger sprockets to the rear wheel, or smaller chainrings at the front. If you change the block at the back to a 12–27, the difference between gears is

large, so that it is very difficult to find the right gear on a climb. You may be over- or under-geared, with no chance of finding the right rhythm.

The alternative is to fit a compact chainset. These have become popular with sportive riders in the last few years. These typically have 50- and 34-tooth rings, and combined with a 12–25 block at the rear, should bail you out of all but the very worst situations. More importantly, they also allow you to spin a lower gear and save energy.

Right: A compact chainset gives flexible gearing in most situations and is invaluable for sportives with long climbs.

Above: On the steepest hills, it doesn't matter how strong you are – you'll need to fit a low gear in order to be able to pedal up.

Maintaining energy levels

As sportives are long events, refuelling should be a vital part of your strategy. Start by eating a large meal with plenty of carbohydrates the evening before, followed by a substantial breakfast on the morning of the event. Carry some snacks that you can eat during the ride: try bananas, energy bars, dried fruit, sandwiches and anything that you find palatable during exercise. Drink plenty of water and energy drinks during the ride, especially on a hot day.

Left: Eating carbohydrates, such as pasta, produces more energy before a sportive event.

Climbing in a Sportive

Many sportive events include significant climbing. Organizers love climbs because they split the field up into manageable proportions, and riders love them for the challenge. With careful planning beforehand, you can turn the hills to your advantage.

Climbing hills on a bike is so difficult and energy intensive that by focusing your training and planning on going uphill as fast and as efficiently as possible, you can make a big difference to the success of your ride. That does not mean you can ignore other aspects of your cycling, but it is on the climbs that the most time can be lost – and gained.

Hill profiles

As part of the preparation for your sportive goal, check the profile to see how many significant climbs there are, and how difficult each one is. Some organizers even provide a detailed breakdown of the climbs, with average gradients for each kilometre ridden. This knowledge is a powerful weapon in your sportive-riding armoury – if you know that a 10km (6 mile) climb has 6 steady kilometres followed by 4 steep kilometres, you know not to overdo it in the early part of the climb and can

Below: Planning ahead and conserving energy when necessary is the best way to climb hills in a sportive event.

Above: When climbing in a group, follow your own pace to the top.

therefore save some energy for the difficult part. If the steep part comes at the bottom, it is a good idea to pace yourself carefully until the climb levels out a little, then go harder with the knowledge that it is not going to get any steeper.

Pace yourself

The frequency and positioning of the climbs will also make a big difference in your planning. The Auvergnate sportive, in France, has four significant climbs, crucially, two of them come right at the beginning. This is too early for heroics, so careful riders will pace themselves well on these two climbs.

Going hard right at the start of a sportive, especially uphill, might lead to an energy crash later. The Auvergnate's two hardest climbs come much later on – it is important to save energy for these two challenges.

Once you are on a climb, and you have an idea of the gradients, your fitness and your physical state, you can get on with tackling it as efficiently as possible.

Apart from physical strength and fitness, climbing well involves being able to focus and concentrate while relaxing. Relaxing sounds like the last thing you should do during such hard work, but while the legs turn, and the body provides an anchor for them to do so, the arms should be nice and relaxed, holding but not gripping the bars.

The right rhythm

Climbing is physically demanding: it hurts, and it can drain your resources incredibly quickly, but if you are able to remain focused and relaxed you can get into a good rhythm, which is what climbing is all about. This is easiest to establish on a steady climb, but it is still also possible on climbs that change in pitch every few hundred metres. Basically, the right rhythm is the one that

Above: On the steepest grades, reduce your speed accordingly – a constant effort up a hill is more efficient than a constant speed.

gets you to the top as fast as possible without going into the red zone (going too hard, then becoming very tired very quickly). The only way to really learn this is through experience. Use a pulse monitor if necessary, but it is better to learn to listen to the way your body feels so that your experience can tell you if you need to back off or go harder. This takes time but can be achieved.

Above: When making a long climb, pay constant attention to what your body is telling you and try to keep to your ideal rhythm.

Once you have established what feels like the right rhythm, sometimes it will take you all the way to the top. However, you must be focused enough to realize if you are going too fast or too slow, even if it is by a microscopically small degree. In this case, just try to alter your effort level a little, slightly up or down, and settle into the new rhythm.

On a climb that is constantly changing in pitch, you have to be able to maintain the same rhythm. This can be achieved by using the gears. Aim for the same pedal cadence and pulse rate by changing down on steeper sections, and changing up on shallower gradients.

Below: The profile of the climb at Mont Ventoux, in gradient percentages. The road to the summit has an average gradient of 7.6 per cent and is one of the most difficult and notorious climbs in the Tour de France.

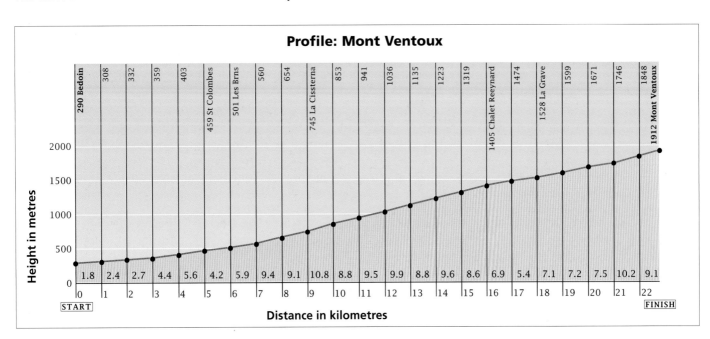

Profile: Mont Ventoux

Riding a Sportive in a Group

On the start line of a sportive, you are sharing the road with up to several thousand other cyclists. It is unlikely that the group will ride round the entire course in one block, but by learning to ride in a smaller group, you can save a great deal of energy and time.

Cyclists riding in a group are faster than individuals riding on their own. The reason for this is that one of the biggest obstacles moving a bike forward is wind resistance. In a headwind, this resistance is made even worse, but it will have significantly less effect if someone is in front of you.

Efficient riding

By cycling behind another rider, it is estimated that you can save as much as 30 per cent of the effort he or she is making for the same speed.

What this means is that a group can work together efficiently and maintain a very high speed with less expenditure of energy. If a group of 12 riders spreads into a line and each takes a turn at the

front before moving to the back of the group, they will only spend a twelfth of the time riding into the wind, which is the hardest part. The rest of the time they are moving to the back of the group, which takes less energy, or sitting in the line sheltered behind another rider. In an hour, if everybody is sharing the workload equally, an individual will only have to spend 5 minutes on the front. That is a lot easier than riding into the wind on your own for an hour. The

Right: Riding on your own is less energy-efficient than riding in a group.
Below: When you are riding a sportive in a group, share the work by taking turns at the front, where the air resistance is greatest.

Above: Pace yourself and ride with others of similar ability, especially in a long sportive. Riders in a group who work out a formation will find that they can cut down their finishing time as well as increase their speed.

Tactical sportive riding

In the last few pages, we have emphasized that riding to your own pace is the best way of ensuring maximum performance and that going into the red zone can have a detrimental effect on energy levels later in the ride. (Going into the red zone is the equivalent of starting to sprint when out jogging.)

There are some occasions when other factors come into play. Imagine a situation where you are about 50m (165ft) from the back of a group near the top of a long hill, and riding at a rhythm which you know through experience is the right one to get to the top efficiently. You are better off riding at your own pace than trying to catch up faster riders. However, if they are only just ahead of you, it's worth chasing them down if there is a flat section after the descent.

By riding in a group, you will save energy in the long term and it will be worth the initial effort to catch them up for the effort you will save by sharing the workload.

If you are in the opposite situation, 100m (328ft) ahead of a small group of riders, it may be best to slow down and wait for them. If you are about to ride a long flat section, there is no point riding hard to hold them off – they will be riding far more efficiently than you, because they are sharing the workload. Instead, grab a bite to eat, sit up a little, stretch and wait for them. You will save a great deal of energy this way.

The guiding principle for sportives is: you are on your own on the climbs and descents, but co-operation with others on flat sections can make the difference between gold and silver awards.

technique of sharing the workload in the group is known as through-and-off, or drafting. It is not a simple case of riding in a straight line. Wind direction makes a difference, as do the relative abilities of the riders in the group. The wind is rarely a zero degree headwind blowing right into your face. More often, with changes in road direction, it is a crosswind and comes from one side or another. The technique for riding in a crosswind still involves riding in a line, but riders also spread out laterally, with the first rider in the group on the side from which the wind is coming. The second rider sits behind him or her, and also to one side, with the following rider taking a similar position and so on down the line. The front rider does his or her turn at the front, then goes back down the line to the back. And so on. This is an efficient way of riding, no matter how strong the wind, and if you join a strong group during a sportive, especially during the flat sections, it will make a difference to your finishing time.

Above: When there is a crosswind, riders form a lateral formation for energy-efficient riding.

Above: When a group rides into a headwind, one rider takes the front position and others spread out behind.

Above: In a smaller group, riders take it in turns to lead, while the others shelter behind the leader.

Descending in a Sportive

Some sportive organizers add to the cyclist's agony by finishing their events at the top of a hill. For all other events, what goes up must come down – for every mountain climbed, there is a descent waiting on the other side.

A lot of time can be lost on a descent. Nervousness about high speed and cornering can cause riders to overuse their brakes. They may also tense up, which makes it harder to flow through corners following the correct line.

Of course, the consequences of going out of control on a descent are far greater than on the flat or riding uphill. Speeds are much higher, so crashes are potentially far more dangerous.

By gaining confidence and relaxing, the descending involved in a sportive should be one of the most fun parts of the ride – and it hurts less than climbing.

Before you even start descending, the most important thing is to have trust in your bike. If it is well maintained, with sharp brakes, and correctly inflated, unworn tyres, you are reducing the chances of something going wrong. If your bike starts to rattle while you are going at 60kph (37mph) down a hill

because it has not been maintained, it is a problem. Second, you must have confidence in yourself and your ability to relax, focus and choose a line.

The shortest line

On a descent where the corners are not that sharp and you can see all the way through, just follow the shortest line down possible (without straying to the other side of the road). Allow your speed to rise to a point where you are totally confident of being able to handle it. If you find yourself starting to go faster than is comfortable, just feather the back brake to check, but not substantially reduce, your speed.

Your bike needs hardly any steering to get round these kinds of corners – shift your weight in the saddle, using your body to turn the bike, and just apply a little pressure to the handlebars to ease the bike through the turn. As

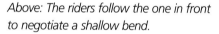
Above: The riders follow the one in front to negotiate a shallow bend.

your confidence rises, you will find yourself wanting to brake less. You will also relax, and start to lean your bike a little more as you round the corners. This is good, but don't relax to the detriment of your concentration – keep looking ahead for sharper corners or obstacles.

When descending, be aware of other competitors and road users and what is going on around you, and try to anticipate what others in front of you will do. If you are unhappy descending, drift to the back of your group so you can follow the other riders' lines through the bends. If somebody in front of you is going too slow, hang back until the right moment to go past them.

Left: When taking part in sportives in mountain areas, safe descent is vital.

Rounding a hairpin bend

1: *Enter a bend from the wide angle.*

2: *Lean over and cut into the corner.*

3: *Hit the apex with outer leg straight.*

4: *Swing out again after the apex.*

5: *Accelerate out of the bend.*

Hairpin bends

Descending becomes more complicated when the corners are sharper, as often happens in mountain regions. Engineers build roads with many hairpin bends, and getting around one of these losing as little speed as possible involves sound technique and steady nerves. As you approach a hairpin, you will probably be travelling quite fast. Keeping the same speed as you round the corner will result in a crash, so you have to check your speed. It is important to start and finish your braking before you start turning, or you risk your wheels locking and throwing you off the bike. The quickest way round is to enter wide, then lean your bike over and turn so that you pass close to the apex of the corner, then exit wide. Using the whole road is the way to maintain maximum speed, but if you cannot see through the corner, do not cross to the other side of the road as there may be oncoming traffic. If the way is clear, use a little more of the road, but safety should be your first concern.

As you turn, keep your inside leg up, point the knee towards the corner and put your weight on your outside leg, but don't be tempted to lean your whole body too far over. By keeping your head erect, you will hold your body upright enough to avoid toppling over. As you start to exit the curve, you can bring your inside knee back in, and you are ready to exit the corner.

By cornering on a hairpin bend, you have lost speed, and if you want to get to the bottom as quickly as possible, it will be necessary to accelerate hard once you are riding in a straight line again. With the gradient helping you, it won't be long before you are back up to full speed and ready to start braking for the next bend.

Applying Your Skills in a Sportive

Never go into an event without thoroughly researching the route. By doing your homework and analysing the distance and profile you can work out the best way for you to ride the race, and thus plan your training accordingly.

Riding a sportive successfully should be part of a long-term, goal-orientated strategy. The sense of satisfaction achieved by planning the build-up to an event, carrying out your training plan and riding the event successfully, is immense. If you surpass your expectations the sense of achievement is all the greater, and even if you are faced with unexpected challenges, dealing with them without panicking can also add satisfaction. Check out events well in advance in cycling magazines and websites.

Using the example of the Marmotte sportive in France, which takes in several Alpine climbs, a plan can be devised for the build-up, training and riding of the event to illustrate how these long-term goals can be achieved.

Research the profile and distance

Before starting the training and thinking about how to ride, you need to research the distance and profile of the event. In the case of the Marmotte, it is 174km

Above: Ride your target event at your own speed. Don't be pressured by anyone coming up behind you.

La Marmotte
Start Bourg d'Oisans, France.
Finish L'Alpe d'Huez.
Distance 174km/108 miles.
Number of significant climbs Four.
Total length of climbs 71km/44 miles.
Vertical height gain 5,000m/16,400ft.

(108 miles) long, which is above average. Your long training rides will have to be lengthened to prepare your body for the extra time in the saddle.

The profile of this event is intimidating. There are a few flat opening kilometres, followed by the long ascent of the Col de la Croix de Fer. The climb looks difficult – it is 27km (17 miles) long, averages a 5 per cent

Left: Train regularly in the months leading up to your target event. It will pay dividends during the competition.

gradient, and tops out at 2,068m (8,550ft) altitude. There is also a downhill section halfway up the climb, followed by a very steep upward incline. When riding, it will be important to pace yourself on the lower section to save some energy for later. Then you can rest on the descent before you reach the second section.

The descent of the Croix de Fer is nice and long – plenty of time to relax and save a bit of energy. It is followed by quite a long flat section to the foot of the next climb. During this part of the ride it is important to get into a group to save energy, and worth waiting for a group if there is none ahead of you.

The Col de la Télégraphe is the next climb – 12km (7.5 miles) long and less steep than the Croix de Fer, with less variation in gradient. It is important to establish a rhythm early on this climb, and make minor adjustments if you start to get tired or feel you are going too slow. The steepest part is at the top, so you might have to reduce speed in order to make the same effort for the final section of the race.

The descent of the Col de la Télégraphe is only a few kilometres long – not enough time to recover significantly, and with the 18km (11 miles) of the Col du Galibier approaching, it makes it all the more important to pace yourself sensibly on the Télégraphe.

The Galibier starts steadily, but gets steeper at the top. Pace yourself at the bottom, even if it feels like you are holding back. Then you will have more energy for the top half.

From the top of the Galibier, there are more than 40km (25 miles) of descent, which is an excellent opportunity to recuperate. This stretch takes you all the way to the foot of the final climb to L'Alpe d'Huez. There are 14km (8.5 miles) uphill to go, with the steepest section at the bottom. Pace yourself sensibly there, then establish a steady rhythm once the climb gets less steep.

Do the training
The training you need depends on whether your goal is to win the event, to achieve gold standard or silver standard, or just to finish the event. You also need to tailor your training according to your experience and ability if you are to achieve your goal.

Whichever category you fit into, the training for the Marmotte needs to be extensive and regular.

Over a period of several months, you'll need to do at least one long ride each week, building up so that you can comfortably handle the distance. To prepare for the climbing, it will be necessary to practise riding uphill as much as possible. A great way of getting yourself into shape for a sportive is to ride another sportive. Why not find one about a month before the Marmotte to test your fitness and practise your pre-ride routine?

Ride the event
The Marmotte is long and hard, but with suitable preparation and training it should not hold any surprises for you.

The main thing to remember is to moderate your pace at the beginning of the route, especially during the first flat kilometres, where it is easy to get carried away and ride too hard.

Try to stay in a group for the flat sections, pace yourself carefully on the climbs and stay relaxed and focused for the descents.

Below: The profile of the Marmotte shows that there are some very steep and difficult inclines to climb.

Above: Train hard over a few months before your chosen event. Practise on similar terrain, especially riding uphill.

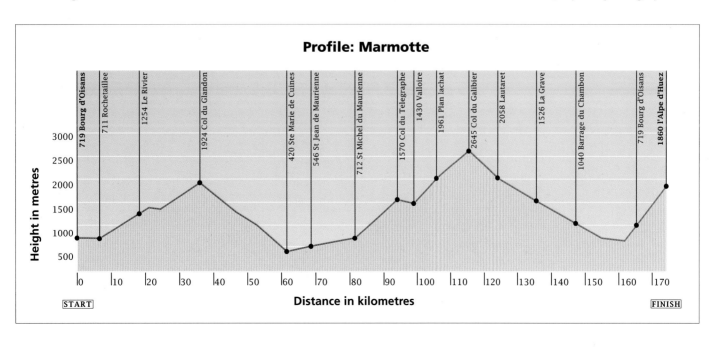

Profile: Marmotte

Height in metres / Distance in kilometres

START — FINISH

Great Sportives of the World: The Etape du Tour

The Etape du Tour is one of the most popular sportive events in the world. Each year, thousands of competitors ride a single stage of the Tour de France, during which they cross some of the most difficult mountains of the race.

The Tour de France is most renowned for its mountain stages. The fastest and fittest cyclists in the world compete with each other on the slopes of climbs such as the Col du Galibier, L'Alpe d'Huez and Mont Ventoux.

Since 1993, amateur cyclists and sportive riders have also been given the opportunity to compete on a Tour de France mountain stage in the Etape du Tour. Over the years, it has become a globally important sportive event, with 8,000 cyclists taking part.

More than 2,000 of these riders come from outside France. Most are from the United Kingdom and the United States, but some of the cyclists come from as far afield as Japan or New Zealand. The organizers of the Etape du Tour, who also organize the Tour de France, want to make their event as spectacular as possible, and they often select one of the hardest stages of the actual race for the Etape route. With few exceptions, they favour stages from the Alps or the Pyrenees, involving the celebrated climbs of the race.

Because there are so many participants, the riders start in waves, counting around a thousand. Entry criteria are stringent, and there are cut-off points along the route – if you ride too slowly, you will be prevented from finishing the event. But while the rules are strict, the satisfaction to be gained from completing the Etape is immense, with the added bonus that you can compare your time with the professionals, who will ride the same course only days later.

A mark of how fit the actual Tour riders are is that the fastest Etape rider is often still an hour or so slower than the last-placed professional.

Tactics for the Etape

Unlike the Marmotte sportive, or the events in the following pages, the Etape follows a different route every year, which means that the preparation and tactics alter from event to event. The 2008 edition from Pau to Hautacam included a long, flat opening section, followed by two difficult climbs (the Col du Tourmalet and Hautacam), while the 2004 edition had a whole series of smaller climbs over the course of a long distance.

Meanwhile, the 2006 edition was one of the hardest in the history of the event, with three of the hardest climbs of the Tour de France – the Col d'Izoard, the Col du Lautaret and L'Alpe d'Huez – on the route.

On a route like that of the 2008 Etape, the biggest temptation would be to start too fast on the fast flat roads in the first half of the event. Pacing is even more important than usual when the end is harder than the start. The route also includes two smaller climbs early on – it's important to take obstacles like this easily, to prevent the build-up of fatigue. On the other hand, the first major climb, the Col du Tourmalet, is harder than the final climb. This means that it might be possible to make a bigger effort on this ascent, knowing that the final climb won't be as bad. However, the tactics for the 2007 event would

Left: The Etape du Tour is one of the most famous sportives in the world – it follows the same route as a Tour de France stage.

have been very similar to those of the Marmotte. With three major climbs en route, including an uphill finish, pacing needs to be steady and conservative.

In spite of its difficulty, or perhaps because of it, entries to the Etape are oversubscribed. Participants from outside France must enter through designated organizing companies, and provide a medical certificate. But if you are fit, and keen to emulate your heroes in the Tour de France, the Etape is one of the most rewarding sportives in the world.

Above: The huge popularity of the Etape du Tour is evident from this picture taken in 2004. The numbers have grown year on year, and as many as 8,000 riders from all over the world now take part. The route varies each year but it is always a difficult one.

Year	Mountain range	Start	Finish	Distance	Climbs
			The Etape du Tour in recent years		
2008	Pyrenees	Pau	Hautacam	156km/97 miles	Col du Tourmalet, Hautacam
2007	Pyrenees	Foix	Loudenvielle	199km/124 miles	Col de Port, Col du Portet d'Aspet, Col de Mente, Col du Port de Balès, Col de Peyresourde
2006	Alps	Gap	L'Alpe d'Huez	193km120/ miles	Col d'Izoard, Col du Lautaret, L'Alpe d'Huez
2005	Pyrenees	Mourenx	Pau	179km/111 miles	Col d'Ichère, Col de Marie-Blanque, Col d'Aubisque
2004	Massif Central	Limoges	St Flour	239km/149 miles	Col de Néronne, Col du Pas de Peyrol, Col d'Entremont, Plomb du Cantal

Great Sportives of the World: Flanders and the Ventoux

The Tour of Flanders is one of the most famous professional bike races in the world. The climb of Mont Ventoux is among the best-known ascents in the Tour de France. It's possible to tackle both in the form of a sportive.

The Tour of Flanders and the Mont Ventoux sportives are a good challenge for ambitious amateur cyclists. Both cover the routes of well-known bike races, although they are very different in their challenge and character.

The Ventoux sportive is similar to the majority of this kind of event – it covers large climbs and is extremely arduous. The Tour of Flanders is different – because it takes place in Belgium, it therefore cannot include

Above: The Tour of Flanders attracts many amateur riders who want to follow in the tracks of their professional cycling heroes.

high mountain passes. But it still remains an extremely challenging and tough event.

The Tour of Flanders
Unlike the Tour de France, which is a stage race taking place over three weeks, the Tour of Flanders is a single-

day event. Flanders, in Belgium, is probably the most cycling-obsessed region in the world, and thousands of fans turn out to watch the race, which happens on the first Sunday of April.

While the Tour de France has its mountains, Flanders has its bergs – these are small but very steep climbs that range between 300m (984ft) and 3km (4 miles) in length, and often have a cobbled surface which makes riding them extremely difficult. Although the route alters slightly most years, there are always between 15 and 20 bergs, which are packed with fans on race day.

The day before the professional event, there is an amateur event over the same roads. The professional race is 270km (168 miles) long, which is an extremely tough proposition, even for fit amateurs, so the organizers also run a 140-km (87-mile) sportive.

Weather conditions are often difficult in Belgium in early April – the Tour of Flanders is traditionally run over flat roads which are extremely exposed to crosswinds. Rain and cold also make it a challenge. Tactically, to do well in the Tour of Flanders sportive, you must be skilled at riding in a group, to minimize the effect of the wind. If the wind is coming from ahead, ride directly behind the rider in front. But if the wind is coming from either side, move to one side of them, so that you are protected.

The climbs also take a special technique, especially in wet conditions. The cobbles are bumpy and slippery, and the steepness of the hills means that traction is easily lost. Usually on a steep hill, standing up on the pedals is the most efficient way to the top, but on slippery cobbles, stay seated, keeping your weight over the back wheel to stop wheelspins from happening. And ride in a low gear, to prevent stalling – the steepest of the climbs are around 25 per cent (one-in-four) gradient.

The Ventoux

The 'Giant of Provence', as Mont Ventoux is known, is one of the most arduous climbs regularly used in the Tour de France. It rises 1,912m (6,273ft) above sea level in Provence, and is all the more impressive for its isolation – it towers above the surrounding hills. Mont Ventoux gained infamy in the Tour de France when British cyclist Tom Simpson died of heatstroke, exacerbated by performance-enhancing drugs, on its slopes during the 1967 race. Ventoux is also famous for being one of the few mountain stages in the Tour de France that seven-times winner Lance Armstrong never managed to conquer.

Above: The Tour of Flanders in 2007 attracted many spectators to watch the professionals ride by.

The Ventoux is a hard, steep climb, with a summit very exposed to wind and sun. There are three roads to the top. The Ventoux sportive is an annual event which takes place in the early summer. It starts and finishes in Beaumes-de-Venise, and is unusual in that the route crosses the climb twice – once from the hardest side, which starts in the town of Bedoin, and once from the easiest side, which starts to the east in Sault. The route includes hilly sections between the two main ascents, and a final 30km (18½ miles) with two significant climbs. The route is 170km (106 miles) long, so it is hard even for the fittest cyclists. This means that tactics for the Ventoux need to be carefully planned. The first 30km (18½ miles) are flat and fast – it is easy to go too hard here, so instead, find shelter in a group of riders and take it easy to the bottom of the first ascent of the Ventoux, which is the hardest part of the course. The climb from Bedoin to the summit of the Ventoux is consistently steep, and 23km (14 miles) long, which means that it takes most amateur cyclists at least an hour and a half to climb it. Too hard an effort here will result in fatigue later.

Right : The mountainous route of Mont Ventoux is so steep and long that even professional cyclists find it difficult.

The final 7km (4 miles) take riders above the treeline, where they are exposed to the hot sun on clear days, and often strong winds. The descent of the Ventoux is one of the fastest in any sportive in the world, but following it, there are 50km (31 miles) of rolling roads where it is easy to go too hard. On both the initial climb and this section, save a bit of energy for the final climb of the Ventoux, up from Sault. This climb is less steep than the approach from Bedoin, but fatigue makes it as hard, or harder than the first climb. And you still need to save energy for the final 30km (18½-mile) stretch to the finish.

If you wish to enter the Ventoux sportive, go to the event's website, at www.sportcommunication.com.

Great Sportives of the World: Cape Argus and Gran Fondo Gimondi

Two of the most popular sportive events in the world are the Cape Argus Cycle Tour and Gran Fondo Felice Gimondi. One takes place in South Africa, the other in Italy, and both are renowned for their dramatic scenery.

Sportives are not just a physical challenge. One of their main attractions is that they take place in spectacular locations, in the mountains, in often beautiful settings. Many events, including the two described here, are a perfect combination of leisure, enjoyment and challenge.

Cape Argus Cycle Tour

This event happens in March, and it is the biggest sportive in the world. Unusually, it takes place outside Europe, in South Africa, with a route that skirts the Cape Peninsula in Cape Town. The event, which started in 1978 with 525 cyclists, has now grown to attract 35,000 entrants who include elite international athletes at the front, covering the 100km (62-mile) route in under 2½ hours, through serious amateurs, to leisure cyclists looking for a personal challenge.

The biggest attraction of the Cape Argus Cycle Tour, aside from the privilege of sharing the road with the biggest group of cyclists in the world, is the breathtaking scenery along the South African coast. The press photographs of

Below: Cyclists climb Suikerbossie Hill in the annual Cape Argus Cycle Tour.

thousands of riders snaking along the coastal road of the peninsula, which is closed to traffic for the day, are so impressive that they attract great public interest in the sport of cycling.

The Cape Argus differs most from the traditional European sportives in the difficulty of the route. It's hilly, but by no means mountainous – the highest point of the event is under 200m (640ft) above sea level. This means that it is more

Above: The Cape Argus Cycle Tour is the world's largest individually timed race.

accessible to leisure cyclists. And at 100km (62 miles), it can be achieved by anyone who has done a little training.

There are five main hills, and many smaller rises along the route, which are steep, but are mainly under 4km (2½ miles) long. Entrants can thus ride in a different way than in the big mountain sportives of Europe. Along the flat roads of the coast, riding in a group will help enormously, by providing shelter from wind resistance. It's also possible to ride at a much more even speed, which makes judging overall pace much easier. Don't start too hard, but the route is not so difficult that you need to save yourself specially during the early stages.

Gran Fondo Felice Gimondi

While the Marmotte and Etape are very hard, events like the Gran Fondo Felice Gimondi are the perfect balance of physical challenge, and rideable terrain.

Climbs of the Gran Fondo Felice Gimondi				
Climb	**Length**	**Altitude**	**Height gain**	**Average gradient**
Colle dei Pasta	3.8km/2 miles	406m/1,340ft	140m/1,340ft	3.7%
Colle Gallo	7.5km/5 miles	763m/2,518ft	426m/1,405ft	5.7%
Selvino	11km/7 miles	960m/3,168ft	653m/2,155ft	5.6%
Forcella di Bura	20.4km/13 miles	766m/2,528ft	613m/2,023ft	4.5%
Forcella di Berbenno	4.5km/3 miles	663m/2,188ft	273m/901ft	5.3%
Costa Valle Imagna	9.5km/6 miles	1,014m/3,346ft	715m/2,360ft	6.6%

The Gimondi, which starts and finishes in the cycling-crazy town of Bergamo in Italy, has six significant climbs, the highest of which is about 1,000m (3,200ft) in altitude. Rather than the steep 25km (15½-mile) slogs of the Alps, these are much smaller climbs, which offer a reasonable challenge without being too tough. At 163km (101 miles), the distance is about average for a big international sportive.

The Gimondi is an interesting study in how to ride a sportive. The climbs vary in difficulty. The Forcella di Bura, which is the fourth climb of the day, is over 20km (12 miles) long, but only has an average gradient of 4.5 per cent, whereas the Costa Valle Imagna, the final climb of the day, is less than half the distance at 9.5km (6 miles), but is much steeper at 6.6 per cent. Each climb demands a different effort, and it is important in this event not to ride too fast on the early climbs. The Colle dei Pasta, which is the first climb, is more of a warm-up for the later climbs, but the second and third hills, the Colle Gallo and Selvino, are increasingly longer.

The final climb is the hardest, which means that pacing is very important – there are five chances to go too hard earlier in the ride, and it is usually better to resist the temptation and reserve plenty of energy for the end.

Right: Two riders cycle home after taking part in a sportive event.
Below: The Gran Fondo Felice Gimondi is a major sportive event, named in honour of Felice Gimondi, a notable professional racing cyclist in the 1960s. He won three Grand Tours, one of only four cyclists to do so.

Great Rides of the World: The Great Races

You don't have to enter a sportive event to experience the great races of the world. Sometimes, it is enough to go and just ride them as a one-day event. All you need is a map, a bike and no small amount of energy and enthusiasm.

At the Etape du Tour, you can ride a stage of the Tour de France. The Marmotte, Gran Fondo Felice Gimondi and Ventoux sportives all offer the chance to compete against thousands of other cyclists on some famous cycling routes. But it's also possible to just go and ride the routes of some of the great races without having to enter a sportive. Road racing takes place on roads which are open to the public for the other 364 days of the year, and it's possible to ride any of them.

Milan–San Remo

Known as the 'Sprinters–Classic', the route of Milan–San Remo is mainly flat, along the northern Mediterranean coast of Italy. As a result, sprinters, who are generally big, strong, heavy riders who are less good at climbing hills, dominate the race history. The best part to ride is the final 100km

Below: The champion, Eddy Merckx, won the prestigious Milan–San Remo seven times.

(60 miles) of the race, or more if you are fit enough. The route is a pleasant ride, with only a few hills to deal with. The most difficult are the 6km (4-mile) Cipressa and 4km (2.5-mile) Poggio, in the final 30km (18.5 miles) before the finish, but they are well-surfaced and steady.

Milan–San Remo
Where to stay San Remo.
The ride Savona–San Remo (110km/68 miles).
Climbs Capo Mele, Capo Berta, Cipressa, Poggio (max altitude 240m/780ft).
Other rides in the area Head inland from the coast to explore the quiet hills.

Paris–Roubaix

Most cycling events get their difficulty from hills. However, Paris–Roubaix is one of the flattest races in the professional cycling calendar. It gets its toughness from several sections of cobbled farm track, which have bumpy and unpredictable surfaces and are extremely

---

Paris–Roubaix
Where to stay Valenciennes.
The ride Valenciennes–Roubaix (110km/68 miles).
Climbs No significant ones.
Other rides in the area Cross over the Belgian border to explore the Chimay.

---

difficult to ride on. The best preparation for riding on the cobbles is to modify your bike so it will absorb as much of the shock as possible. You will need thicker tyres, and stronger wheels if possible. Professional cyclists put two layers of bar tape on, to make gripping the handlebars easier.

When riding the cobbles, maintaining speed is very difficult, but crucial if you are to avoid getting knocked off your line. Stay relaxed and vigilant and try to look a few metres ahead at all times,

Below: The roads of the Paris–Roubaix race are as challenging and difficult as any mountain pass.

Above: The cobbled track in the Paris–Roubaix event is very hard to ride on.

Above: Italy's Paolo Bettini is a former winner of the Tour of Lombardy.

so you can spot any large cobbles that jut upwards. This kind of surface takes a lot of getting used to.

Liège–Bastogne–Liège

A more traditional cycling challenge is Liège–Bastogne–Liège – its difficulty comes from a succession of long and steep climbs winding through the forests of the Ardennes in Belgium. The race starts from Liège, and heads down to the turning point at Bastogne. It's a good idea to pick it up from here – the hills are almost exclusively in the second half of the race. None of the climbs are

> **Liège–Bastogne–Liège**
> **Where to stay** Bastogne.
> **The ride** Bastogne–Ans (150km/93 miles).
> **Climbs** Many, including the Côte de Stockeu, Haute-Levée, Redoute and Sprimont.
> **Other rides in the area** Head west to Huy to ride the famous Mur climb, which features in the Flèche Wallonne race.

longer than a few kilometres. But their steepness and repetitive nature sap the energy from the legs. One good idea is to fit a compact chainset, so that you have a wide selection of low gears.

Tour of Lombardy

The climbs of the Tour of Lombardy, in Italy, are in some of the most beautiful cycling country in the world. They are long, moderately steep, and offer a good physical challenge. The route circles Lake Como, and covers 260km (162 miles). Even missing the first part of the race and riding from Como involves 220km (137 miles) of hilly riding – it's probably best to divide it into two halves, and stop over in Parlasco, on the west side of the lake.

Approach these climbs like mountain roads – it's important to establish an early and good rhythm, because if you go too hard too soon, you will suffer in the final kilometres. The most famous climb of the Tour of Lombardy is the Madonna del Ghisallo, with a chapel at the top, filled with cycling memorabilia.

Left: The peloton starts in Liège for the Liège–Bastogne–Liège challenge ride.

> **Tour of Lombardy**
> **Where to stay** Como.
> **The ride** Como–Como (220km/136 miles).
> **Climbs** Parlasco, Colle di Balisio, Madonna del Ghisallo, Civiglio, San Fermo di Battaglia.
> **Other rides in the area** The hills around Lake Como are some of the best for cycling in the world.

MOUNTAIN BIKING

Mountain biking is one of the most beneficial and fun exercise regimes you can follow. While road riders have to share the road with traffic, on a mountain bike you are generally in splendid isolation, in beautiful surroundings, on challenging terrain. It doesn't even matter if it rains. While bad weather can be demoralizing for other forms of cycling, wet weather is all part of the fun of mud-plugging (off-road riding). There are many different disciplines to try out on a mountain bike, from trail riding and downhill riding to freeriding.

Above: Learning how to ride safely down a steep hill is a vital skill.
Left: Mountain biking through a forest on a rocky road will help to improve your fitness, while being extremely enjoyable.

Choosing a Mountain Bike

With such a wide range of off-road bikes available, it can be hard to choose what type to buy, let alone a specific model. When buying a bike your needs, budget and ambitions all have to be taken into consideration.

Before taking the plunge to buy a bike, you have to decide whether you want a specific bike for a specific task, or a more versatile model to allow you to explore more than one branch of off-road cycling.

Specific bikes are easy to decide on. If you want to ride trials, only a trials bike will do – the specification is so exact and developed that a normal mountain bike will be unable to meet performance needs. You really need a downhill bike for cycling down hills properly. It is possible to ride down some courses on a hardtail bike with suspension forks, but

Right: For trials riding, you'll need a specialized bike.
Below: A full-suspension mountain bike is suitable for heavy-duty off-road riding.

you will have to keep your speed so low to cope with the bumping and shock that it will detract from the fun.

If you decide that you are going to ride off-road, then you need a more general bike, and this is where the massive choice starts to get confusing. You might be more specific, and decide that you want to race cross-country, but then you have to choose between hardtail and full suspension, V-brakes or disc brakes, even between eight- and nine-speed freewheels.

For those who just want to enjoy the occasional bit of trail riding, a hardtail bike with V-brakes and suspension forks will probably return the maximum benefit. A bike like this is versatile enough to be ridden on the trails and make it a rewarding experience, but it is

Above: A downhill bike is designed for one purpose only – it's too heavy to ride back up a steep slope.

not so specialized that it can be used only for this purpose. There is also the advantage that it can be used as a runaround urban bike and fulfil that function perfectly well.

If you are going to take the sport more seriously and hit the trails on a regular basis, perhaps embarking on longer challenge rides, your equipment needs to be a bit more specialized.

There is no easy answer to the hardtail versus full suspension debate – the topic has been debated for years. All you can do is make your own decision, based on what you think you will get out of each type of bike.

If you are light and good at climbing, you might consider going for the full suspension – the extra weight will slow you down on the hills, but as you climb fast, you can afford to slow yourself down marginally. On the other hand, when it comes to bowling down the other side of the hill, the full suspension will allow you to maximize your speed and efficiency. Likewise, an occasional

rider who prefers a bit of light trail riding on a warm day might not need to install disc brakes, when V-brakes will do just as well. If you are planning to go out in all weathers throughout the year, disc brakes are probably the right option. The most important thing is to

Above: Hardtail mountain bikes are good for off-road riding, and are more efficient for all-purpose riding.

work out which bike will give you the most enjoyment and let you cycle effectively.

The Hardtail Bike

Hardtail mountain bikes are light and fast and handle precisely, and they are excellent for speed and efficient climbing. The front suspension provides comfort and control of the bike and the fat tyres allow smooth riding on roads.

A basic mountain bike, either with suspension or regular forks and a normal aluminium frame, is known as a hardtail. Although full-suspension bikes are currently popular for their greater shock absorbency in bumpy conditions, a traditional hardtail can still be the best bike for basic cross-country and trail riding. They are lighter than full-suspension models. They also have the advantage that, combined with slick tyres, they make a far better road bike. When buying a mountain bike, it is easy

Right: Gear shifters are located on the handlebars for quick changing.

Anatomy of a hardtail bike

❶ Frame: Aluminium frame, compact, but with plenty of clearance for fat tyres. Skinny seatstays absorb much more impact.

❷ Fork: Suspension fork for shock absorption and a more comfortable ride on rough and bumpy surfaces. Most forks can be adjusted for shock absorbency, depending on the type of terrain.

❸ Wheels: 32-spoked wheels, with 26in rims, which are smaller than those on a road bike. Width can be 1.5–3in.

❹ Tyres: Thick and knobbly for extra grip on loose surfaces.

❺ Chainrings: Triple chainrings offer more possible gears.

❻ Sprockets: Eight or nine, depending on preference and model.

Much wider spread, to give very low gear options for steep hills.

❼ Brakes: V-Brakes for greater stopping capacity than regular callipers. Disc brakes are becoming more popular for their efficiency in all weathers.

❽ Gear shifters: Integrated into brake system for ease of access.

❾ Saddle: Comfortable, supportive saddle, good for rough terrain.

Trials bike

Trials bikes are an offshoot of mountain bikes used for jumps and riding over obstacles, either artificial or natural. Riders keep their feet up, and ride, hop and jump from obstacle to obstacle, balancing on the super-fat tyres even when the bike is not moving.

A trials bike has a very short seat tube, which enables the body to move over the bike and perform a jump called a sidehop, in which the bike jumps both up and laterally. The frame is very stiff and responsive, with no need for energy-absorbing suspension. Riders gain control from a wider set of flat handlebars, which give more leverage.

Wheels are usually 26in, with fat tyres at low pressure to grip surfaces. A single small chainring, usually fitted with a guard to protect it from damage when it hits an obstacle, is combined with a seven-, eight- or nine-speed freewheel. Brakes need to be very strong – many riders choose hydraulic systems, which lose less power than a traditional cable. Some riders don't even use a saddle on their trials bike – the jumps are all executed standing up.

to be impressed by the sophisticated technology of full-suspension designs, but depending on your needs, hardtail mountain bikes are resilient and reliable. Hardtails are more sensitive to accelerations, giving a more responsive ride, which purists and traditionalists prefer. For general fitness riding and enjoying getting out on the trails, a basic hardtail model with eight-speed freewheel and V-brakes is a good choice.

Frames and components
The majority of hardtail frames are aluminium, and they are compact and low. A long seatpin, small frame and 26in wheels, which are smaller than road wheels, keep the rider's weight low to the ground. This makes the bike more controllable at low speeds, either going up steep hills, or dealing with highly technical sections. Riders often have to jump off their bikes, and a low top tube makes this easier.

The triple chainset, with chainrings with 42, 32 and 22 teeth, plus an eight-speed freewheel is a good combination for riding your mountain bike over a

Above: Disc brakes are powerful enough to check speed even on loose surfaces and down steep hills.

variety of terrains. On very steep hills, which you can often encounter on a trail ride, the inner chainring should be able to deal with the gradient.

Brakes can be either disc or the traditional V-brakes, depending on what you want to get from your riding. Disc brakes perform better in bad

Above left: Suspension forks and disc brakes help control your bike.
Above: Chunky tyres are necessary for off-road riding, to aid grip.

conditions, and overall, offer more stopping power. V-brakes are simpler and lighter.

Full-suspension Cross-country and Downhill Bikes

In recent years, the technology of full-suspension frames has improved significantly. For trail riding, the full-suspension bike gives a much more comfortable ride, which is especially important when riding long distances.

Bumps and shocks tire and bruise the body – riding a full-suspension bike can reduce these shocks and make the experience of trail riding positive and even more enjoyable.

Full-suspension bike

There is no doubt that riding a full-suspension bike down hills is easier than on a hardtail, on which all the bumps you ride over are transmitted straight to your saddle area. The suspension irons out the lumps and bumps, giving a faster, more comfortable ride.

The payoff for the extra comfort, however, is reduced speed and extra weight. Full suspension adds a few kilograms to the weight of your bike, because of the extra tubing and machinery involved in the suspension system. Every time you ride up a hill, you will be carrying more weight than a

Below: Full-suspension frames make for a less harsh ride over bumpy ground.

Above: Keep your mountain bike clean and well maintained – riding off-road in poor conditions can wear down components very quickly.

traditional hardtail, and the efforts quickly mount up and can tire you out. However, the more technical the terrain, the more the full-suspension bike comes into its own. So over the course of a long ride, including uphills, downhills and technical sections, the full suspension will probably have a net benefit effect on the speed of your ride.

Downhill mountain bike

With most other types of mountain bike, riders always have to compromise between speed and comfort. The downhill mountain bike is designed purely to absorb bumps and shocks. Downhill mountain biking has its roots right back in the origins of the sport. The first mountain bikers were the Californians who rode general-purpose bikes down Repack Hill in the 1970s, and the tradition has continued to the present day, when the downhill is a major event in the World Cup series, attracting huge crowds with spectacular races. Downhill cycling is a time trial from the top of a hill to the bottom, with bends, jumps and steep straights on which riders can reach massive speeds, sometimes over 95kph (60mph). The downhill bike, more than any other, relies on strong suspension with a great deal of travel (amount of give in a suspension system) to absorb the shocks at speed. It also needs to be manoeuvrable – courses often include sharp bermed (high-sided) corners and narrow sections that demand great control, even at speed.

Frames are full suspension, with lots of travel and large springs to absorb the impact of bumps that are hit at 80kph (50mph). The fork suspension travel is enormous, since it is the front wheel that takes the brunt of the hits. Controlling speed effectively means that disc brakes are the only real option, as they have a larger braking surface than regular mountain bike V-brakes. The chain is kept in place with a retainer, and the chainring is protected.

The riding position on a downhill bike is not over-streamlined, in spite of the fact that aerodynamics are important. The saddle is kept low, to keep the rider's weight close to the ground and the bike stable.

Above: The travel on full-suspension bikes can be altered depending on the terrain you expect to encounter.

Anatomy of a full-suspension cross-country bike

❶ Full-suspension frame: Provides greater shock absorbency, and greater control and traction in rough terrain.
❷ Suspension fork: Takes all the impact where the bike feels it most – at the front wheel.
❸ Brakes: Disc brakes are essential for better stopping power at speed and

for cycling in poor conditions such as mud and water, bumpy surfaces and rocky roads.
❹ Wheels: Rims are 26in with 32 spokes for lightness and strength. Width is 1.9 or 2.1in, for the right balance between grip and rolling resistance.

❺ Tyres: Thick knobbly tyres grip the ground in rough terrain.
❻ Gears: Nine-speed freewheel, combined with a triple chainring with 22, 32 and 42 teeth.
❼ Pedals: Reversible clipless pedals so that the shoe can clip into either side of the pedal.

Clothing and Equipment

The varied conditions experienced when out mountain biking mean it is a sensible idea to wear specialized clothing that will minimize discomfort. Comfort is a priority as well as protection from the cold and wet.

In the summer, clothing is simple. A pair of shorts, plus a base layer for your top, and a loose cycling jersey are the most comfortable option. Some mountain bikers wear skin-tight Lycra road-racing shorts, while others prefer the look of baggy shorts, but be careful of catching them on your saddle as you stand up on the pedals. Jerseys do not need to be as tight fitting as those of road riders, since speeds are lower and aerodynamics less important. A loose-fitting jersey will help keep you cool.

Gloves are essential. No one is immune from crashing, and you will need to protect your hands and fingers if you stack your bike. Full-fingered gloves are advisable for off-roading.

Helmets, too, are just as important for off-road riding as they are on the road. If you come off, you could be seriously injured if your head hits a rock or tree roots.

If you are not planning on having to put your feet down, you can use stiffer-soled shoes similar to those of road cyclists. However, most mountain bikers will want the kind of shoe that clips into your pedals, but is also comfortable and

Above: Extreme conditions make it necessary to wrap up warm.

flexible for walking. For steep sections of trail you may need to dismount and walk, and it helps to have some grip.

In winter it is important to dress well because of the wet conditions. Depending on how mild or cold it is, you may need a windproof and waterproof jacket. Even if it is not raining, water can still spray up off your companions' wheels. Long leggings will keep your legs warm and shoe covers will protect your feet from the elements. A warmer pair of gloves and a hat are also useful. Even when the sun is not shining, it is a sensible precaution to wear goggles to protect your eyes.

Left: A lightweight waterproof jacket will protect you from the rain.
Right: Keeping feet warm is important.

Mountain bike tyres pick up mud and stones and sometimes they can be flicked up into the face of the rider behind.

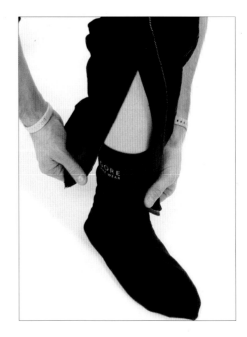

Above: Baggy winter clothing is warm and practical for off-road riding.

Above: If speed is important to you, Lycra leggings are more aerodynamic.

Above: In summer, shorts and a long-sleeved top will protect you from scratches.

Full-face helmet

Shoulder pad

Padded jacket

Shoulder pad

Elbow pad

Flexible padded gloves

Knee pads

Padded shorts

Shin pads

Downhill body armour

Downhill racers need serious protection for their bodies, in case of a crash.

On your head, you need a full-face helmet. It is not enough just to wear an ordinary hard shell helmet – these do not protect the face. A comfortable and effective full-face helmet will protect the whole of your head, as well as the back of your neck. Cover your eyes with goggles that fit inside the opening of the helmet.

Body armour will protect your arms, legs and body. Parts of your anatomy tend to hit the ground more than others and these parts have extra-hard shell protection. The knees and shins have a hard shell, as do the shoulders, elbows, wrists and chest. Downhill crashes tend to cause injuries from skidding along the ground, Full body armour, however is specifically designed to minimize this damage.

Padded downhill gloves are flexible, to allow you to control the brakes and steering without loss of sensitivity, while for your feet, protective shoes with thick soles help when you put your feet down in the corners.

Trail Riding Skills: What to Expect

Riding a mountain bike along a trail is exhilarating and fun, but it also requires concentration and a good skills base. By practising your technique, you can make your off-road riding a much more rewarding experience.

The very best mountain bikers rarely bounce along bumpy trails, they glide and flow. This is the riding style you should aim for – relaxed, efficient and comfortable. By shifting your weight around subtly, finding the right line and letting the bike do some of the hard work, you can start to ride with more economy.

Each different kind of surface demands a slightly different approach, but there are some general rules and techniques to apply to your riding that can help you improve. These involve keeping momentum, absorbing shocks and keeping your weight back.

On rough surfaces, it can seem as if the bike is fighting you and trying its best to stop. These surfaces can cause inexperienced riders to lose speed, and the slower you go over or through an obstacle, the harder it becomes to deal with. So try to maintain momentum into, through and out of especially

rough patches. Try not to hit obstacles at maximum speed, but keep a positive pedalling action and pick your way through trying to lose as little speed as possible. Losing speed means using more energy to keep going.

Shocks

Absorbing shocks is an important part of maintaining momentum. When you hit a loose surface or technical section, sometimes the reaction is to try too hard to control the bike, which makes your body tense and stiff. Relaxed arms and legs are natural shock absorbers, and if

Left: On extreme descents, keep your weight back as far as possible.

Above: When descending, keep your weight over the rear wheel for traction and balance, while at the same time lightly braking.

you can absorb the bumps, your progress will be smoother.

Lastly, your bike will react better to the terrain if more of your weight is over the back wheel. If you hold your weight too far forward, steering is compromised on rough terrain. Putting your weight over the back wheel increases traction while pedalling and will give you more control over your speed. Your front wheel should be free to manoeuvre, but should not be so loosely held that it bounces around.

Muddy conditions

The more sticky the mud is, the lower the gear you will need. Sit well back and maintain traction. Pick your line and try to stick to it, keeping your weight off the front wheel so that if it starts to get stuck you can easily pull it out before it sinks and pitches you off. You should be able to ride over the rocks, but hitting them at a bad angle knocks the front wheel out of alignment, affecting momentum and steering, so plan ahead

to follow a line that avoids bigger stones. The ride is bumpy, so stand up and bend your arms; the arms and legs act as shock absorbers. In most off-road situations, spinning a low gear is better than pushing a large gear, but in rocky terrain, a larger gear is better to try to maintain speed and momentum. If you are deflected into a new line by bigger rocks, follow that new line. When you steer, use your body and hips to help to change line.

Riding over roots

Roots are present on many off-road trails. In wet weather they usually become slick, and if you hit them at the wrong angle, you can take your bike out from under you, even if you have fitted rugged tyres. The way to tackle roots is to hop the front wheel over them, avoiding wet roots if possible, then use the back wheel to generate speed to pass over them in a straight line, at a right angle to the root.

Dealing with mud and rocks

Mud: *Put the bike into low gear. Pick a line and try to stick to it.*

Rocks 1: *Follow a line and plan ahead to avoid large stones.*

Rocks 2: *Stand up in the saddle so that the legs and arms absorb the shock.*

Dealing with roots

1: *Approach the roots and plan a path through them.*

2: *Hop the front wheel over the roots. Beware of wet, slippery roots.*

3: *Pass over the roots at a right angle to the direction of growth.*

Trail Riding Skills: Choosing a Line

Riding in a straight line is easy but the challenge of mountain biking involves the unpredictable nature of the trails. Being able to pick your line, anticipate problems and corner fast and safely are important skills.

When riding, it is natural to look just ahead of the front wheel, so that you can deal with problems as they arise. But looking farther ahead is far more efficient – that way, you can avoid problems before they happen, rather than have to deal with them.

Look ahead

Pick your line well in advance. When you can see a rough patch approaching, look for a suitable entrance point, a good line through, and a possible exit. That way, you have already ridden the section in your mind before you actually get to it on the bike and will be prepared for each stage. Sometimes you may have to change your tactics if your original line turns out to have a hidden obstacle, but that is all part of the fun and challenge of mountain biking.

Looking ahead can help with gear selection, too. If you get caught out by a sudden steep rise it is easy to stall, but if you have changed down already in preparation for a climb, you will be ready to ride all the way up.

Right: Even when pedalling uphill out of the saddle, it's still important to concentrate on controlled steering to get you safely up.
Below: Allow your bike to steer for you by following the natural line of the trail.

Above: Be prepared to take action if you come to a sudden corner on a singletrack.

Singletrack

Riding singletrack is one of the most rewarding off-road cycling experiences you can have – it tests your reflexes, fitness and bike handling.

Singletrack is just that – a one-lane mountain bike trail wide enough for one bike at a time. It twists and turns unpredictably, and has all the variety of surfaces that off-road riding has to offer. Often they come unexpectedly –

Above: Use your upper body to help steer your bike, leaning into the turns to aid traction.

you may dive out of a sharp corner only to discover a large rock under your front wheel or find yourself up to your hub in mud. Riding singletrack is a matter of ducking and diving around the corners and being able to deal with obstacles that come when you least expect them. Singletrack demands a much more erratic speed than larger trails. You will very often have to brake sharply for corners, then accelerate out of them. The aim is still to maintain flow, but within the bounds the singletrack imposes on you.

To control speed in twisting sections, use the back brake, and manoeuvre the bike using both body weight and turning the handlebars. Use the front brake for sharper stopping. You'll need to change gear often as the speed alters. Because of the need to accelerate, it is better to spin a lower gear and anticipate changes down so that you are ready to speed up again.

Cornering

An important skill in mountain biking is cornering quickly and safely. There are very few trails that travel in a totally

Left: Always try to anticipate what is coming up when riding at speed.

straight line – you'll be constantly turning and changing your line during the course of a ride.

Cornering involves three phases – the approach, the turn and the exit.

In the approach, use your brakes to moderate your speed. The aim is to enter the corner as fast as possible without the risk of overshooting. As you enter the corner, lean your body over to counteract the centrifugal force, and stay seated. This allows you to push down on your outside leg while bending your inside leg away from the bike for extra balance. Keep your weight centred over the bike, spreading it equally between the front and back wheel to maintain grip.

Once you are past the apex, your aim is to accelerate out of the corner. As soon as you have rounded the bend and can see your exit point, start to pedal.

On a smooth corner with a banked surface, your speed can be high all the way through. Be prepared to slow down more for gravelly surfaces, adverse cambers and other obstacles.

Above: Accelerate out of tricky situations to prevent getting stuck in a rut.

Trail Riding Skills: Descending

Descending is theoretically the easiest thing about trail riding on a mountain bike. Gravity pulls you downward, and all you do is control the bike by keeping your weight back. Then just relax, steer, brake a little and enjoy the ride. But it takes skill, too.

Your main priority when descending is safety. On shallow descents this is straightforward – keep a laid-back position, and use the brakes when you need to. Look well ahead and plan your line. If the surface gets bumpy and you have a hardtail bike, stand up on the pedals to let your legs act as shock absorbers.

Steep descents involve a little more care. You need to be aware of your centre of gravity, and be more focused on the movement of the bike underneath you. Your line should be the shortest one, surface permitting, so cut corners tightly.

Keep your weight back when descending – too much weight above the front wheel can move your centre of gravity far enough forward that you become unstable. The steeper the descent, the farther back you need to sit. Once it becomes really steep, you can hang off the back of the saddle with

Right: Keep weight back when descending to prevent tipping over forwards.
Below: When descending, use your arms and legs to support your body weight.

Right: Keeping your weight above your back wheel helps maintain traction and allows you to react to obstacles.

your bottom above the rear wheel. In this position, your centre of gravity is still low enough to keep you stable, but pay attention to your steering.

Finding a way down

Steering on the descents is easier if you shift your weight and lean rather than turn the handlebars. This is all part of being relaxed and letting the bike do the work of finding its own way down.

On a slippery or loose surface, descending becomes more complicated. Overusing the brakes can result in a crash, so the best technique is to moderate your speed before you hit the gravel. Unless there is particular difficulty ahead, don't brake on a loose surface, but if you have to, keep your weight well back, your centre of gravity low, and feather the brakes so that you regain control.

Drop-offs

On some off-road descents, mountain bikers can encounter drop-offs, which are vertical drops in the path or trail. Some are so small that you might not even notice them, but others are quite dramatic and take a lot of practice before you can deal with them confidently. To ride a drop-off, you don't need to be riding fast, but it helps if you are riding positively and confidently. Do not use your brakes once you are committed to the move.

On the approach, move the bike into a straight line and put your weight slightly over the rear wheel. As the front wheel goes over the edge, pull your handlebars up, bending your arms, and stay back over the rear wheel. Your rear wheel should hit the edge, and your momentum should cause both wheels to land together at the bottom of the drop-off. Your bent arms will take some of the shock of landing.

During the final approach, look at where you intend to land and plan your exit strategy so that you don't lose momentum.

Drop-offs

1: *Put your weight over the rear wheel and pull up the handlebars.*

2: *Look ahead and decide where you are going to land.*

Trail Riding Skills: Climbing

Climbing is an unavoidable, and difficult, part of trail riding. It is part of the huge variety of terrain you can come across, even on just a single ride, and being able to do it effectively will make your ride a more positive experience.

The steepness of a hill dictates how you tackle it on a mountain bike. On a shallow incline, it is just a case of sitting comfortably, with your body stretched out as you ride to the top. On steep climbs, or climbs with loose surfaces, technique plays a significant part in getting up.

Relaxation is also important. Instead of bunching up your entire body and holding the handlebars in a death-grip, concentrate on breathing evenly, open out your chest a bit, and hold the bars firmly, towards the outside. If you have bar-end attachments, use those to stretch yourself out a bit.

Maintain traction

When the surface of the climb is loose, keeping traction is the biggest challenge. A wheelspin can slow your progress almost to a halt, so to ensure it

Above: When climbing steady gradients off-road, stay in the saddle and sit back, spinning a low gear.

doesn't happen, sit back and keep your weight over the back wheel. At the same time, to keep your centre of gravity low and increase traction in both wheels, stretch out so that your body is almost parallel to the top tube.

Loose surfaces can also affect your bike when you are standing up and pedalling up a hill. If you sway your bike from side to side, as sometimes feels natural, you run the risk of it slipping out from underneath you. Try instead to move your body from side to side, keeping the bike upright beneath you.

On a very steep climb, with your weight back, it is possible for the front wheel to come off the ground and cause you to lose momentum. On a steeper climb, move your weight forward a little, consciously maintaining traction in the rear wheel.

Golden rules of climbing

1 Stay in the saddle

Climbing is all about establishing a rhythm, and the easiest way to do this is to relax and focus, and stay in the saddle. Grip the bars firmly but not tightly, settle your weight where it feels comfortable and effective, and climb with good rhythm. Save standing up for where you have to accelerate, or stretch out your legs.

2 Bend forward, stretch yourself out, keep your weight back

When climbing, rear-wheel traction is everything. Keep your weight back over the rear wheel to prevent it slipping, but stretch forward with your upper body to get a lower centre of gravity. This will also help traction.

3 Use a low gear

It is less tiring to your muscles to spin a low gear fast than try to turn a big gear over. By staying in a low gear you will have more energy later on. Also, changes in gradient can slow you down – if you are already pedalling slowly you run the risk of stalling.

4 Change the numbers

You can climb faster without even having to go out riding. Climbing effectively is all about power-to-weight ratios. So spend some time and effort, and money if necessary, on losing weight, both you and your bike. Then do some specific hill-climbing training to boost your power. Your climbing will improve out of all recognition.

5 Take the easiest line

The easiest line is not necessarily the shortest one. Corners are often much steeper on the inside than on the outside. The extra distance on a shallow gradient can be less tiring than the short distance up the inside with a steep gradient.

Climbing

Sit down: *Most of your climbing should be done sitting down, with the weight over the back wheel for traction.*

Weight back: *If necessary, stand on the pedals on steeper gradients, but keep the weight back.*

Side to side: *When climbing, move from side to side. Keep the bike straight, to prevent it slipping out beneath you.*

Stand up: *Standing up on the pedals stretches the legs, helps combat tiredness and gives a little extra acceleration.*

Weight forward: *On the steepest climbs, move your weight forward a little for traction with the rear wheel.*

Keep going: *Maintain your speed and effort to the top of the climb to prevent stalling.*

Downhill Racing

Taking part in a downhill race is not as easy as just sitting back and freewheeling while the bike does all the work. It is a serious athletic challenge, and all mountain bikers should have a go at it – it is fast, exhilarating and fun.

On the face of it, downhill riding looks like the easy option for mountain bikers. Dressed from head to toe in protective body armour, riders plummet down steep paths on bikes that look more like motorbikes. If they want to go down again, they catch the ski-lift back up to the top. This isn't simply laziness; downhill mountain bikes are so engineered that they weigh a great deal more than normal bikes, and riding back up would be very difficult.

Downhill riding takes a cool head, nerve, co-ordination and skill. It also takes physical strength – on well-designed courses riders rarely freewheel. Instead, shallower gradients and sharp corners require fast riding and acceleration to maintain velocity.

Your first few downhill runs should be more about gaining confidence and getting used to the way a downhill bike handles. Get used to the brakes and acceleration, and then ride a bit harder. Preparation on a downhill run is essential, and it's worth walking the course to inspect it before you ride. By getting a mental picture of the right line to take, and where to brake, when it

does happen it will be more natural. Actually riding the correct line is a matter of experience and anticipation. By looking well ahead of your front wheel, you will be in a position to choose the right line.

Corners and jumps

The start of a downhill ride is an important part of the whole descent. The margins of victory in competitive downhilling are often very small, and the difference can be made in the initial acceleration. A powerful sprint out of

Left: Full protective body armour is absolutely essential for anyone taking part in downhill racing.

Above: Riders can reach incredible speeds on the steepest gradients in downhill events.

the starting blocks will give your ride physical momentum. It is also a statement of intent – by starting as fast as you mean to go on you can give yourself a psychological boost. Once you are into the ride, you can deal with the sections as they come.

Most corners have berms, which help you to maintain your line through them. When you approach a bermed corner, brake before you start to turn, then hit the berm on the top half. Lean over and shift your body weight on to your outside pedal, which should be down,

and following the line should be straightforward. Follow these steps and your cornering will be a lot faster and better controlled.

Some corners don't have berms, and the best technique is to use your lower leg in the corner for balance. Riders come round some corners so fast that their bike is almost horizontal, with their leg skidding around on the floor to keep them upright, and to help the bike around the corner before getting it upright again. Use longer, straight

Above: At the start of a downhill race, acceleration is all-important, and riders sprint out of the gate.

sections to build up speed, but be careful of your exit – if you fly too fast into a technical section, you can crash. Some sections will be quite flat, and it's important to try and sprint through these, in order to maintain your speed.

At certain sections, there are small jumps. Hit these jumps with your wheels straight, lift the front wheel up, closely

Above: Hitting a ramp at speed means riders can jump. It's vitally important that the bike is straight for landing.

followed by the back wheel, and be careful to land straight. Look ahead while you are making the jump, so that the exit from your landing is as safe and speedy as possible.

The most important and useful skill to develop, along with your confidence, is your ability to let yourself and the bike flow down the hill. Your reactions to the course have to be fast and fully committed.

Left: Cornering at speed on a berm. Below: During flat sections, the rider holds speed by pedalling hard and maintaining an aerodynamic tuck.

Freeriding

A recent development in mountain biking is freeriding, which is perhaps the ultimate expression of the sport. It is an improvisatory way of combining cross-country riding, downhill riding, trails and trick riding.

The inspiration for freeriding initially came from snowboarders. Freeriding in snowboarding takes place off-piste, away from the beaten track; mountain bike freeriders do the same. Sometimes freeriding involves building jumps and narrow wooden walkways to ride on. Often it is a case of finding your own trail and using logs and rocks.

The definition of freeriding by the sport's originators in British Columbia is that there is no definition.

There is an element of downhill riding, but freeriding also involves riding through more technical terrain. While downhill riding involves getting from A to B as quickly as possible, freeriding means getting from A to B in as stylish and innovative a way as possible.

Freeriding has provided cycling with some of its most photogenic moments since its development at the turn of the century. Freeriders have sought out steeper drops to ride off, and they build ever larger jumps. The original freeride trails incorporated narrow walkways 3m (10ft) in the air. These days the walkways are 12m (40ft) off the ground.

A freeriding bike is very like a downhill bike. The frame is heavy duty with full suspension, although as it often

Right: Freeriders build their own obstacles, putting narrow walkways up to 12m (40ft) off the ground.
Below: Huge jumps are an integral part of freeriding, with the best riders finding ever larger drops to ride.

Above: Freeriding bikes have full suspension, with enough travel in the front forks to absorb impact off jumps.

has to be ridden up hills and for longer distances, it is not as bulky. Its wheelbase is shorter and the head tube is steeper, which gives more control when performing jumps.

Special bike features

The long travel suspension forks have been retained from downhill bikes – freeriding involves dropping off obstacles and jumps, and the shock of

landing needs to be taken in the forks. Disc brakes with a large braking surface also survived from downhill bikes – landing off a 3m (10ft) cliff involves a fair amount of acceleration, and speed might need to be checked very quickly.

Unlike a downhill bike, however, the freeride bike has a triple chainset and therefore a larger range of gears. The

Left: Freeriding courses often incorporate narrow log beams, which test the riders' balance to the limits.

Above: There is no limit to the complexity of freeriding courses.

greater variety of terrain expected to be encountered by a freerider also requires the gears to deal with it.

Freeriding involves elements from many mountain bike disciplines: the trick-riding abilities of the trials rider, the reflexes and nerve of the downhill rider, the physical strength and urge to explore shared by all trail riders, and the competitive instincts of the racer.

Mountain Biking: Branching Out

Mountain biking isn't just about trail riding and cross-country. There are a multitude of other racing and riding disciplines that are challenging and fun, including bicycle four-cross, slalom, trials and dirt-jump riding.

Mountain biking is primarily about having fun, and there are a variety of disciplines outside cross-country riding. Four-cross and slalom are action-filled races over short distances including jumps, berms and downhills. Trials riding is more technical – it's all about hops, jumps and tackling obstacles. Dirt-jump riding is an underground scene with the emphasis on style and expression.

Four-cross

At a bicycle four-cross event, four riders start at the same time, and race to the bottom. Bikes are full suspension, with short seat tubes and low saddles like a trials bike, and crashes are common. Riders need nerves of steel and great technical ability to ride down a steep section of hill with jumps and corners, elbow-to-elbow with other riders. Speed alone might not be enough – races are often decided by the jumps, and course designers keep the suspense alive to the finishing line by incorporating as many unpredictable elements as possible.

Slalom

A type of racing that involves two riders going head-to-head on two near-identical but separate courses down a hill is

Above: Bicycle four-cross is a fast and furious race on specially designed courses, with four riders going elbow-to-elbow in a downhill dash to the line.

'slalom'. Originally, it was simply erecting the poles in a field and letting the riders go, but it evolved into an organized part of the sport. The course became more technical, with jumps and berms between the slalom poles. With the development of the 'dual' slalom, in which riders start separately, until their lanes merge, there was more conflict. Once you have established a lead in an event like the slalom, it is easy to keep it, so a typical race sees aggressive fighting to reach the merged lanes in first place.

Trials

Another form of mountain biking, trials, entails performing tricks and jumps over a series of obstacles. In trial biking

Left: In a slalom race the bikes ride down separate but identical courses.

Trials riding: jump

1: *A rider starts to jump off the top of an obstacle.*

2: *In mid-air, the rider positions his bike to effect a good landing.*

3: *The rider is not allowed to put his feet on the ground.*

competitions, riders have to negotiate a set course without putting their feet down, or allowing any part of their bike apart from the tyres to touch the obstacle. If they do, they are penalized. There is also a time limit, and when riders exceed it, they gain a penalty point for every 15 seconds taken over the limit.

Below: Four-cross courses can incorporate jumps taken at great speed to try to gain an advantage over rivals.

Trials riding takes great skill and balance – riders can use their strong brakes and soft, grippy tyres to balance on their rear wheel and hop on to obstacles up to 1.5m (5ft) in the air.

Dirt-jump

One of the more underground areas in the sport is dirt-jump mountain biking. While other riders go off in search of obstacles, part of the process of dirt-jumping is building your own. This has

led to clashes between dirt-jumpers and landowners who have recently discovered that there is an unapproved dirt-jumping track on their land. Like freeriders, dirt-jumpers insist that their sport is not about competition but free expression. The aim is not to be the fastest, or the highest, or even to be able to perform the best tricks, but simply to execute a jump in a way that feels natural and expressive to the individual rider.

Great Mountain Bike Rides in Canada: North Shore and Whistler

North Shore, in British Columbia, is one of the world's major centres for mountain biking. Initially it was a well-kept local secret, based around Mount Seymour, Mount Fromme and Cypress Mountain. Whistler has hundreds of mountain bike trails.

The North Shore is endowed with challenging trails for singletrack riding, while Whistler has trails for every ability.

North Shore

Now regarded as the home of freeriding, North Shore, with its jumps, ramps and elevated trails offers some of

Below: British Columbia is a major area for cross-country mountain bikers.

	British Columbia Bike Race		
Stage	**Start**	**Finish**	**Distance**
One	Victoria	Cowichan Lake District	112km/70 miles
Two	Cowichan Lake District	Port Alberni	115km/72 miles
Three	Port Alberni	Comox Valley	83km/52 miles
Four	Comox Valley	Sechelt	60km/37 miles
Five	Sechelt	Gibsons	55km/34miles
Six	Squamish	Whistler	75km/47 miles
Seven	Whistler	Whistler	25km/16 miles

Above: Although there are well-marked trails, many riders choose their own.
Left: The North Shore area was where freeriding developed.

the best and most varied mountain biking in the world and it is legendary in the sport. There are many watercourses and forests with huge trees, and because there are creeks and fallen timber, narrow, high bridges have been built that are often used as launch ramps. The trails at Mount Fromme are easy to explore, although riders are expected to stick to a few rules regarding the trails, other users and the environment. Exploration is in keeping with local traditions – just arrive and see what happens.

Whistler

One of the biggest cross-country trail locations in the world, Whistler has hundreds of kilometres of trails, based at three locations in the area. One of the most famous rides in Canada is the seven-day British Columbia Bike Race, from Victoria to Whistler. Each day involves around 4 to 8 hours riding and a daily distance of 50–100km (31–62 miles). There are seven stages of the ride and the climbing can be exacting. Mud can make the route hazardous. If you have prepared and are in fair shape, you will have a good riding experience.

Right: The cross-country riding in British Columbia is challenging, but the views make the effort worth it.

Great Mountain Bike Rides in the USA: Moab, Utah

Moab, in the south-eastern corner of Utah, is one of the best places for mountain biking in the world, with mile upon mile of trail of every description. Every mountain biker should go there at least once.

The most famous trail in Moab is Slick Rock, a 15.5km (9.6-mile) loop of sandstone rock. While it gains its name from the difficulty of riding horses on the hard stone, for mountain bikers there are few better surfaces to ride on. The sandstone offers unbelievable traction. The original trail is marked out with white paint. The terrain is steep and hard, and set in a Moon-like landscape. While it is short compared to many off-road loops, the demanding technical nature of the course is such that it can take hours to complete.

What makes Slick Rock such a natural place for mountain bikers is that it couldn't have been better designed as a technical mountain bike course. The trail incorporates natural bowls, some with steep sides, which are ideal places to experiment with tricks, jumps, drop-offs and more extreme riding. There are none of the restrictions that define most trails – on a singletrack course you have no choice but to follow the path. On Slick Rock, going off-piste and improvising your own way down is part of the experience.

The other main off-road trail in Moab is the Porcupine Rim Trail, which is less famous than Slick Rock, but has a better reputation among Utah's mountain bike aficionados. It is a 33km (20.5-mile) trail that finishes in Moab and consists of extended stretches of broken rocky singletrack. It is known for the 915m (3,000ft), 18km (11-mile) descent from the top of the first climb all the way

Below: The arid sandstone area of Moab, Utah, is one of the biggest mountain biking challenges in the world.

down to the Colorado River. In Moab there are also dozens of short trails, long trails, hard trails and beginners' trails. One trail, farther from Moab, the White Rim, is based on a 160km (100-mile) loop in the Canyonlands National Park. This ride takes two or three days, and you need camping equipment.

Above left: Although this looks as if it would be extremely difficult, Moab sandstone has superb traction, making technical manoeuvres like this possible. Above: The trails in Moab are highly demanding and technical – riders often have to improvise their way out of difficult situations.

Below left: The desert around Moab is wide open, with plenty of opportunities for easier, less technical riding. Below: With the changing scenery and riding like this, it is no surprise that Moab is now considered to be one of the top worldwide mountain biking destinations.

Great Mountain Bike Rides in Europe

The mountain ranges of Europe are natural playgrounds for the off-road enthusiast. For cross-country and downhill riders, the French Alps and Pyrenees are among the most desirable destinations in the world for off-road riding.

Mountain biking has become a major summer sport in the Alps. Those in the tourism industry have realized that ski resorts can be used by mountain bikers during the summer, and in some areas have made great efforts to design attractive destinations for off-road riding.

Rides in France

In the French Alps, Morzine has become a Mecca for downhill riders with four of the best downhill tracks in the world within a few kilometres of the town. The Les Gets course is used for the World Cup event, while the Super Morzine is one of the longest downhill tracks in Europe. There are many trails for riders of all abilities, ranging from steep and difficult

Above: Morzine offers a huge variety of trails, ranging from easy to extremely challenging. The downhill tracks are among the best in the world.
Above right: The Alps in summer have become a major destination for cross-country mountain biking.

downhills at the top of mountains to easy cross-country trips.

Morzine is also a centre for cross-country riding, with popular local routes into the mountains. The Col de Cou is a steep climb which rises 400m (1,312ft) from bottom to top with a 1,000m

(3,280ft) descent to reward the effort of making the top. Morzine has more than 400km (250 miles) of bike-specific tracks for mountain bikers, but the most interesting proposition for experts is the 110km (68-mile) Portes de Soleil route.

Many of the cross-country rides can also incorporate chairlifts to take out some extended uphill grinds, although for some this is all part of the fun. And whether you pick an easy trail or a serious downhill run, there is fantastic scenery to enjoy.

As well as Morzine, Chamonix, in the shadow of Mont Blanc, has developed many mountain bike trails.

Rides in Spain

Spain has an advantage for mountain bikers, especially in the south, in its good all-year-round weather. The Sierra Nevada mountain range has some of the highest mountain biking in Europe, while the Alpujarras in Andalucía has been described as a cross-country paradise for aficionados.

The Pyrenees are following close behind the Alps as a destination for mountain bikers. The Valle de Tena is located in the western Pyrenees, right on the French border, with a good network of trails, and no restrictions on routing. The Val d'Aran has abundant cross-country trails, and you can create longer routes by including road links.

The Picos de Europa, which is based around Potes, is one of the world's best mountain bike destinations, with challenging trail rides and many long descents.

Top right: The terrain makes mountain biking in Spain a challenging experience.
Right: Many European mountain biking centres have extensive singletrack trails.
Below: Mountain biking in Europe benefits from clement weather all year.

Great Mountain Bike Rides in the UK

There are many fantastic rides in the UK; among the most notable are the trails in the South Downs, Wales and the innovative 7stanes in Scotland, which links seven mountain bike centres in the south of Scotland by a variety of trails.

Although spectacular mountain bike rides in the UK are numerous, a handful stand out. For a long ride, the South Downs Way is unbeatable. Wales is crisscrossed with trails and there are mountain bike centres to help along the route. Scotland, however, is acknowledged as having the most diverse and difficult rides.

South Downs Way

The first national trail in the UK to be designated a long-distance bridleway, the South Downs Way has become a challenge for mountain bikers. It starts in Winchester and follows the South Downs all the way to the coast at Eastbourne. The total length, from end to end, is 160km (100 miles), with 4,150m (13,600ft) of ascent and

descent. The highest point is Ditchling Beacon, at 248m (814ft) altitude. The ride is seen as a serious challenge not for the toughness of its terrain, but its distance. It has become a challenge to ride the entire length in a day, although most people tend to split it into two days.

Rides in Wales

Established as the main area for British mountain biking, Wales has hundreds of miles of purpose-built singletrack and trails shared between the biggest centres at Coed y Brenin forest and the Afan

Right: Empty moorland in Derbyshire is ideal for cross-country mountain biking. Below: This route on the South Downs Way can be tackled in one or two days.

Forest Park. Purpose-built mountain bike centres are a good way of enjoying the sport without the risk of cycling on private land or getting lost. Afan Forest has a network of trails, including the original 22km (13.6-mile) Penhydd trail, which is a suitable distance for ambitious novices and intermediate riders. For more experienced riders, trails such as the Skyline Trail, at 46km (28.5 miles) in length and with 2,000m (6,500ft) of vertical gain, are a substantial challenge.

Rides in Scotland

Mountain bikers in the UK find that Scotland has the most varied and challenging terrain. The low population and mountainous landscape are perfect for long rides and expeditions. Biking centres have sprung up over the last few years, such as the 7stanes network. Trails range from 400m (1,310ft) in length to the 58km (36-mile) Glentrool ride. Fort William has become popular since hosting the World Cup mountain biking events.

Above left: Even in a densely populated country like Britain, there are still some wide-open spaces to explore.
Left: The UK has some of the best and most extensive singletrack riding.

Above: Riders tackle a challenging cross-country mountain biking trail in Afan Forest in Wales.

Great Mountain Bike Rides: Multi-day Events Around the World

For the ultimate mountain biking challenge, many riders are signing up to multi-day events in the great mountain ranges. The TransAlp, TransRockies and Cape Epic Challenges give riders a chance to test themselves against the toughest terrain in the world.

For more experienced riders, multi-day events are increasingly popular. The TransAlp, the TransRockies and the Cape Epic, all with great climbs, are three of the most demanding.

The TransAlp Challenge

An eight-day challenge ride across the Alps, the TransAlp climbs a series of high passes in daily stages ranging between 50 and 100km (30–60 miles). It has run every year since 1998, starting in Mittenwald in Germany and finishing in Riva del Garda in Italy. The routes are a combination of off-road tracks, gravel paths and asphalted surfaces. Some days involve a height gain of over 3,000m (9,842ft). It is an extremely arduous race, one of the most difficult mountain bike events in the world. Riders have to be fit and follow an advanced training schedule to prepare. Such is the popularity of the TransAlp that more than 500 teams take part every year.

2008 Route TransAlp Challenge Ride				
Stage	Start	Finish	Distance	Altitude gain
1	Füssen	Imst	80km/50 miles	1,962m/6,437ft
2	Imst	Ischgl	76km/47 miles	3,171m/10,403ft
3	Ischgl	Scoul	75km/47 miles	2,547m/8,356ft
4	Scoul	Livigno	77km/48 miles	2,621m/8,599ft
5	Livigno	Naturns	122km/76 miles	2,909m/9,544ft
6	Naturns	Kaltern	97km/60 miles	3,930m/12,894ft
7	Kaltern	Andalo	74km/46 miles	3,071m/10,075ft
8	Andalo	Riva	62km/39 miles	1,480m/4,856ft

2008 Route TransRockies Challenge Ride				
Stage	Start	Finish	Distance	Altitude gain
1	Panorama	K2 Ranch	52km/32 miles	2,478m/8,177ft
2	K2 Ranch	Nipika Resort	74km/46 miles	3,813m/12,582ft
3	Nipika Resort	Nipika Resort	44km/27 miles	1,514m/4,996ft
4	Nipika Resort	Whiteswan Lake	110km/68 miles	2,567m/8,471ft
5	Whiteswan Lake	Elkford	89km/55 miles	2,147m/7,085ft
6	Elkford	Crowsnest Pass	102km/63 miles	2,998m/9,893ft
7	Crowsnest Pass	Fernie	79km/49 miles	2,101m/6,933ft

The TransRockies Challenge

The success of the TransAlp Challenge led to its format being copied around the world, with the Canadian TransRockies Challenge starting up in 2002. The route is still developing, but it can be extremely punishing, and the weather can be variable. Like the TransAlp, the TransRockies is split into daily stages, covering 600km (372 miles) in seven days and climbing a total of 12,000m (39,000ft), a little below the TransAlp, but still a very hard challenge.

The short history of the TransRockies gives a perfect illustration of the unpredictable nature of this kind of event – in 2003 forest fires forced the

Left: Riders negotiate the TransAlp, one of the most difficult bike events.

*Above: Mountain bikers tackle a scree
trail in the Rocky Mountains.*
*Above right: The route of the Cape Epic
is entirely off-road and goes along
rugged tracks, through the beautiful
scenery around the Cape.*

organizers into a swift re-routing
exercise at very short notice, while
the 2004 event was hampered by
heavy rain.

The Cape Epic Challenge
The first event in the South African
Cape Epic Challenge, in 2004, attracted
more than 500 riders for the 800km
(500-mile) route, and within two years it
had doubled in size to 1,000 riders and
increased its length to 921km (572
miles). Every year it starts in Knysna
Waterfront and finishes in Lourensford
Wine Estate. The total climb for the
eight-day 2007 event was 15,045m
(49,360ft), comparable to the TransAlp.

Preparation
Taking part in multi-day events like the
TransAlp, TransRockies and Cape Epic is
not to be undertaken lightly, because
100km (62 miles) is a long way to ride
off-road on a single day, let alone on

2008 Route Cape Epic Challenge Ride				
Stage	**Start**	**Finish**	**Distance**	**Altitude gain**
Prologue	Pezula	Pezula	17km/11 miles	310m/1,020ft
1	Knysna	Saarsveld	123km/76 miles	3,091m/10,141ft
2	Saarsveld	Calitzdorp	137km/85 miles	2,518m/8,261ft
3	Calitzdorp	Riversdale	133km/83 miles	2,340m/7,677ft
4	Riversdale	Swellendam	121km/75 miles	2,620m/8,596ft
5	Swellendam	Bredaarsdorp	146km/91 miles	1,819m/5,968ft
6	Bredaarsdorp	Hermanus	130km/81 miles	2,095m/6,873ft
7	Hermanus	Grabouw	91km/57 miles	1,985m/6,512ft
8	Grabouw	Lourensford	68km/42 miles	1,760m/5,774ft

several days. To get the most out of
the experience, it is necessary to be
honest and realistic about your own
capacities, and to train hard over a
long period to prepare for the event.
Try following or adapting some of
the training programmes in this book
to prepare yourself, and take part in
some shorter events to make sure
that your body can take the longer
distances and repeated efforts of a
multi-day event.

*Right: Many challenging mountain
bike races go through spectacular,
mountainous terrain, such as this one
at Mount Hood, Oregon.*

GETTING FIT

To get the most out of your cycling you need to
put in some hard work. Entering a cyclo-sportive on
the road or an enduro event off-road is easy to do.
But getting yourself into the best possible condition,
in order to do yourself justice in the event, takes
planning and training. You need to train hard, but you
also need to train smart, focusing on strengths and skills.
A series of training schedules are suggested for you to
adapt to your own needs. All the workouts can be done
on or off-road – whatever's most convenient for you.

Above: Establishing a regular training routine is the key to getting fit.
Left: With a little hard work you will be fitter, more energetic, and have more fun.

Fuelling for Cyclists

In order to train effectively, and recover from the efforts you make in training, you need to eat correctly. Training hard takes energy, and before riding you need to ensure that you have consumed enough fuel to get you through.

What you want to avoid is a hunger crash – known in common cycling slang as the 'bonk'. Great name, terrible feeling. Make sure you eat enough before a ride, during it if necessary, and afterwards to allow your body to repair itself and to restore energy levels. However, there are some things that you should resist.

If you aim to lose weight, change your mindset and decide to reduce body fat. By cycling, you are building muscle, which is heavier than fat. Don't use the bathroom scales to assess how healthy you are – instead, monitor your body-fat levels and energy levels. You can buy body-fat monitors that will help you chart your progress. Energy levels are easier to monitor – simply judge whether you feel better or worse.

To lose body fat you need to expend more calories than you consume. But don't be tempted to speed up the process by skipping meals before or after riding. Aim for a more gradual loss of fat, so you can maintain your energy levels, continue cycling and get fitter and stronger.

Below: Drink regularly on training rides to avoid dehydration. You may want energy drinks, but you need water, too.

Quality nutrition

It is important to eat good quality food made from fresh ingredients. A natural diet is worth the effort – your energy levels will be higher, your immune system stronger, and your health will receive a boost. Ready meals, fast food and sugary drinks are loaded with fat, salt and refined sugar. Instead of these, eat plenty of fresh fruit and vegetables, lean meat, pulses, nuts, grains and dairy products. When training, it's important that your diet includes the right balance of the major food groups: carbohydrates (simple and complex), protein, 'healthy' fats, and vitamins and minerals.

Above: Refuelling on the go is an essential part of cycling training. Bananas are easy to carry and pack a lot of energy so are ideal for cyclists.

Carbohydrates

The bulk of your energy should be provided by carbohydrates. They break down into glycogen, which is stored in your muscles and liver before being converted to glucose to provide energy for your muscles. Your body stores enough glycogen for about one and a half hours, so if your training ride is longer, take high-carbohydrate food with you to maintain energy levels.

Far left: Carbohydrates such as bread and grains are needed for energy.
Left: Eating meat and fish regularly will provide protein to help your body recover from the effort of training.
Below far left: Dairy products also provide daily protein.
Below left: Eat as many fresh vegetables as possible to get essential vitamins.

There are two kinds of carbohydrates – simple and complex. Simple carbohydrates are found in foods such as fruit and refined sugar, and are quicker and easier for the body to absorb. However, they often give a 'rush' of energy that can be followed by an energy crash.

Complex carbohydrates are slower to be absorbed, and provide a steadier release of energy. They can be found in rice, pasta, potatoes and other starchy foods. If you are training hard and regularly, it is essential to eat plenty of carbohydrates.

Protein

Some energy is provided by protein, which is also really useful for cyclists in repairing damaged muscle fibres.

Proteins contain amino acids, which rebuild body tissue and help keep your immune system strong. Proteins are found in all meat, poultry, fish, eggs, cheese, nuts and pulses, and to a lesser extent in grains. It is essential for endurance athletes to consume a healthy level of protein, to help the

muscles grow stronger over the course of a training programme. Chicken and fish are generally better than red meat in providing the necessary protein in your diet. Red meat has plenty of protein, but also has high levels of fat. Once in a while is fine; every day is not.

Fat

Although eating too much fat is unhealthy, you still need to include some in your diet. For long rides it is the main source of energy. There is also evidence that it may help in boosting your immune system. Be aware, however, that there are 'bad' fats and 'good' fats. Saturated fat and trans-fatty acids that occur in animal fats are 'bad' fats and should be avoided. Unsaturated fat is 'good' fat, and can be found in products such as olive and sunflower oil.

Vitamins and minerals

To run effectively, the body needs the help of vitamins and minerals. They are found mainly in fruit and vegetables. When you are exercising regularly, your body needs a good supply of vitamins

and minerals, especially vitamins C (in citrus fruits and vegetables) and E (in cereals, seeds and nuts), which reduce damage done to your body and help it to recover. It is also important to keep iron levels up, as iron (in liver, watercress and red meat) enables the blood to carry oxygen efficiently. A balanced diet, with plenty of fresh fruit and vegetables, should provide enough in the way of vitamins and minerals. Getting these through food is the best way. During periods of intense exercise, or when you are tired, a multivitamin supplement can help boost your levels.

Water

Dehydration can occur after training sessions. Drink water through the day, especially during and after exercise.

Typical eating plan

Breakfast
Bowl of homemade muesli with dried apricots, a sliced banana and milk.
Toast with honey, jam or Marmite.
Freshly squeezed orange or grapefruit juice.
Coffee or tea.

Lunch
Salad of fresh vegetables and pulses – lettuce, tomatoes, bell peppers, cucumber, chickpeas, red cabbage, beansprouts.
Add lean meat or cheese.
Bread roll.

Dinner
Grilled chicken with lemon, garlic and olive oil.
Boiled potatoes or rice.
Steamed broccoli or other green vegetable.

Through the day
Drink plenty of water.
Take a vitamin supplement if you think your energy levels are low.
Snack on fruit or breakfast cereal.

Basic Training 1: Endurance

The biggest part of your cycling training will be working on your endurance potential. The more this is improved, the longer you will be able to keep going without getting tired. It needs dedication, but the results make it worthwhile.

Good endurance allows your body to adapt better when you start working on more specific fitness. If you think of your fitness for cycling as a pyramid, the bottom layers are all endurance. The bigger the base of the pyramid, the taller it can be built.

At a basic level, building endurance is simple. By riding your bike regularly, and increasing the distance and time of your rides, you will increase your endurance.

Endurance training workouts

Long steady distance training (LSD) is one of the most enjoyable parts of a cycling exercise programme. It does exactly what it says – an LSD ride involves riding for long periods at a pace you can maintain. How long, how

steady and how far an LSD ride needs to be depend on your own fitness and abilities, and what your aims are. If your long-term goal is to ride a 50km (31-mile) sportive event, it is not essential to train to ride a 100km (62-mile) event, but if you have the time and energy it won't do any harm, and you might be able to set a higher goal. Training rides of 50km will not build enough endurance if your goal is a 100km event.

As for terrain, you can choose hilly routes, flat routes or somewhere in between for your LSD rides.

Right: Regular training boosts fitness. Below: You will perform better in a sportive if your training was specifically targeted for that event.

Just maintain a constant intensity of effort, using between 70 and 75 per cent of your maximum heart rate. If your MHR is 200, riding with your heart rate at 140 to 150 beats per minute is the right level. If you are just starting out cycling, these rides should start at 30 minutes, but you can quickly build up to two hours. Experienced and fit cyclists can maintain this pace for several hours.

Recovery rides

These are similar to LSD rides, but shorter and less intense. After a hard day of training, your body needs to rest and recover and attempt to adapt to the stresses you have placed upon it.

Above: Endurance training should take place at a pace that you can hold for long distances.

A recovery ride will speed up your body's recovery from hard training and flush out waste products from your muscles. If you go out for an easy ride, at low intensity, and over a short distance, your body will be less stressed and will not start breaking down. It will boost your system and raise your metabolism without making you tired.

It's important not to be tempted to go too hard on a recovery ride, even if you feel that you can. Save yourself for when you are rested. Likewise, there's no need to go out for hours – an hour or less turning the pedals at a high but easy cadence in a low gear is the perfect recovery effort. Your pulse should be between 50 and 70 per cent of your MHR, depending on how tired you are. Err on the side of caution for these rides.

As your cycling training and fitness develops, you will learn to listen to what your body wants and decide whether to ride or not. Avoid too much climbing for your recovery rides – it is better to stay within a comfortable level of exertion. If

Left: During some training rides, shorter, more intense efforts will improve your fitness levels.

Working with your heart rate

Your heart rate is one of the most reliable and accessible ways of judging how much effort you are making. By using a pulse monitor, working out your maximum heart rate (MHR), and looking at what physical effort you can maintain at different percentages, you can make your training much more effective.

The traditional way of guessing one's MHR was to subtract one's age from 220, so a 30-year-old man should have an MHR of 190. However, the population varies so this rule is fairly inaccurate. By far the best way of finding out your MHR is to push yourself so hard that you cannot go any faster, then check the readout on a pulse monitor. You may be one or two beats out, but for all except elite athletes, this is an acceptable margin of error. The best way to find your MHR is to go out on a ride, find a hill, and sprint up it at a rate that is unsustainable. Sooner or later, the agony will force you to stop – when this happens, try to squeeze out 5 more seconds of energy. Then push a tiny bit more, and just as you feel like getting off your bike and lying where you fall, look at your pulse rate monitor. It should be showing your MHR.

Above: A heart-rate monitor measures the pulse in beats per minute during exercise.

you go hard enough to get tired, you will be too fatigued for your next workout to be effective.

If you have a recovery ride scheduled but are feeling very fatigued, it may be a better idea to take the day off. Put your feet up so your body can repair itself.

Basic Training 2: Speed

It is fun to be able to ride long distances at a steady pace. It's even more fun to be able to ride fast and vary the pace of your training rides. Riding fast, either sprinting or maintaining an above-average pace for a few kilometres, is what defines cycling as sport.

It is an amazing feeling to be able to accelerate under your own power, especially at the end of a ride. The fitness required to do this demands training and energy, but training like this gains momentum that carries on into your next workout. When you are training hard, and getting fitter and faster, the feeling of improving is a major motivator.

Being able to ride fast as well as steady will add a new dimension to your cycling. It will improve your energy levels and fitness. In a sportive event you will be able to chase a group so as to benefit from their shelter. It could make the difference between winning a gold award and a silver award.

You should embark on speed training once you have established a good base of cycling fitness through endurance rides. Experienced riders have the base fitness to start this type of training after a couple of months of endurance riding. If you are new to cycling, give it a little longer. Remember that fitness is like a pyramid. The bigger your base endurance the higher the peak. When embarking on these training sessions, always warm up thoroughly, and allow enough time for recovery at the end.

Sprints

During a normal LSD ride, put in two or more sprinting efforts. Look ahead for a street sign or tree on a flat road.

Right: Between efforts, pedal easily to recuperate and prepare for your next try. Below: Speed training will enable you to ride harder and longer, which helps in sportive events and racing.

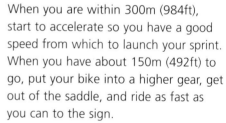

When you are within 300m (984ft), start to accelerate so you have a good speed from which to launch your sprint. When you have about 150m (492ft) to go, put your bike into a higher gear, get out of the saddle, and ride as fast as you can to the sign.

Once you have passed the sign, you can change down gears and settle back into your LSD pace, or a little below if you are having trouble recovering. You don't need to look at a pulse monitor for this exercise – your aim is to go as hard as possible for a short distance, to build speed and strength. Recover for as long as you need to feel relaxed and normal again – at least 10 minutes – then go for another sprint and repeat the procedure. Following this sprint, assess how you are feeling now. If you are tired, carry on at LSD pace for the rest of your ride. If you feel good, do another one, two or even three sprints in exactly the same way.

Left: The fitter you are, the better your performance in a sportive will be.
Above: Professional riders hone their fitness with plenty of speed sessions.
Left: Speed efforts should be at an intensity that is close to your maximum.

Spinning drills

Cycling takes strength, but it also helps if your legs are supple and flexible. The faster you can spin the pedals, the more supple your legs will become.

Once a week, go for a ride and aim to spin the pedals at 100 revolutions per minute or more throughout.

This is difficult to get used to, especially if you are new to cycling, but turning the pedals fast eases the pressure on your muscles.

Tempo riding

Riding faster for long periods of time is called 'tempo riding'. This is an essential part of building fitness for riding enduros as well as competing in sportive events.

Tempo sessions involve riding at a steady pace that will eventually tire you out. At the end of an LSD session, it is good to feel that you could go on farther, but a tempo session should be designed to push you harder.

For your first session, warm up for 30 minutes, then ride for 15 minutes at 75 to 80 per cent of your MHR. This is fast enough to induce discomfort, but at a level that you can hold for the length of the set – in this case for about 15 minutes.

Steadily increase the time you spend at tempo pace in subsequent workouts until you can ride like this for an hour.

Jumps

These are similar to sprint workouts. The efforts are shorter, but involve more repetitions. During an LSD ride, on a slight incline or along the flat, change up into a big gear, accelerate and ride 15 pedal revolutions as hard as you can. Recover for 2 minutes, then go again, four more times. Continue, at a steady pace, for 10 minutes, then repeat the above, with five repetitions. If you feel good after this, do one more set of five jumps.

Fartlek training

Speedplay, or fartlek in Swedish, is a less structured way of adding sprints, jumps and varying tempos to your training.

During a fartlek ride, simply ride hard, steady, all-out or slowly according to the way you feel, and on a variety of terrain. When you reach a hill, sprint over the top. On a long flat section, look for a sign and sprint for it. Then ease off for 5 minutes before riding the next 3km (1.8 miles) at a fast pace. Or do whatever you feel like doing.

Fartlek is good training for the unpredictable way sportives and enduro events can evolve. By incorporating fartlek sessions into your training routine you can get used to changes in pace. If you have been following a strict plan for a few weeks, a varied fartlek session can be motivational.

Basic Training 3: Climbing

Riding fast uphill on a bike is a very specialized kind of physical exertion. It is probably the most painful aspect of cycling for sport, but if you do the appropriate training, it correspondingly offers the greatest sense of achievement.

There is really only one way of improving in the hills: you have to ride a lot of hills. Training for hill riding is hard work, but will have a big effect on your ability to tackle them in an event. Not many people enjoy hill training, but if you can motivate yourself to work hard on your climbing, you will be at a comparative advantage. You will also benefit the rest of your cycling – strenuous training in the hills strengthens your legs and body, and works your cardiovascular system hard. A cyclist who regularly trains hard in the hills is a cyclist whose fitness will increase dramatically.

After you have done a few weeks of the speed workouts, you will be ready to start working on your climbing training. You need to have worked on endurance building to get benefit from these sessions.

Right: When going uphill, climb out of the saddle now and then to stretch you legs and alter your position.

Hilly tempo ride
Design your training route to take in as many hills as possible – repeating some climbs if necessary. Try to avoid long flat sections. Variety of hills is a good thing – if possible, incorporate some short, steep ascents, long steady climbs, and

Above: It is the hills that can test your fitness to the limits.

everything in between. This workout is unstructured along the same lines as a fartlek speed session – just go hard when you reach a climb. Try to spend

most of your time sitting in the saddle and riding in a controlled way. Don't burn yourself out by going too hard, especially at the bottom of the climbs, but ride at 80 per cent of your MHR when you ride uphill. Once you have completed two or three sessions you can start to incorporate short bursts of faster climbing halfway up a hill, or really sprinting for the top. These efforts will take you over 80 per cent of your MHR, but you will start to develop the ability to recover from these efforts and settle back into your tempo pace. Above all, this workout should be fun and free. You can reward yourself for the efforts you put in on the climbs with descending practice on the other side.

Above: Keep a steady effort over the course of a hill, rather than sprinting.

Short steep hill repetitions

Find a hill that has a gradient of about 8 per cent. Warm up, then ride up at a fast pace, about 80–85 per cent of your MHR, for three minutes. Ride in the saddle until you start to feel fatigued, then stand up on the pedals to maintain your pace. When the time is up, stop and turn around, or continue at a very slow pace so you recover completely before the next climb. Repeat this effort. If you are very tired, warm down and ride home. Otherwise, you can do up to four repetitions.

Above: Practise climbing with riders of a similar ability so that you do not overreach yourself.

Long steady climbs

Find a climb that is up to 3km (1.8 miles) in length and is no steeper than 6 per cent. Once you have warmed up, ride at 80 per cent of your MHR, staying in a seated position, for 6 minutes. Practise breathing steadily, relaxing the shoulders and arms, and focus on turning your legs at 80–90 revolutions per minute. Recover completely, then do three or four repetitions depending on how tired you feel.

Hill sprints

Find a short, steep climb that takes a minute to get up at speed. Build up momentum into the climb, then try and maintain your speed all the way to the

Above: There is no substitute for hard effort in the hills during training to boost fitness and strength.

top. The final 100m (330ft) will be very hard, but sprint out of the saddle until you have crested the climb. Recover completely and repeat two more times.

Mountain climbs

If you live in a mountainous area, find a long climb – 5km (3.1 miles) or more, with a 5 to 7 per cent gradient. Spin up in a low gear, staying seated, at 75–80 per cent of your MHR. The aim is to build resistance to fatigue and practise riding the types of climb you will encounter in a hard sportive event.

Below: Climbing the steepest hills is tough, but with determination you will be able to make it to the top.

Weight Training for Cyclists

Cycling is the best training for cycling. If you are planning on entering an enduro, a sportive or a race, there is no substitute for miles on your bike. However, it is a good idea to complement your cycling with other forms of training if you have the time for it.

Weight training is a good method to give yourself all-round body strength, but cyclists should not do too much of this kind of exercise. The more bulk you build through weight training, the heavier you will become, which means more body weight to carry up hills. Don't overdo it.

For the best results in terms of strength, you should focus on three different sets of exercises when you are weight training to improve your performance as a cyclist. These are: leg exercises, which will enable you to ride more strongly; upper body exercises, because the arms have to work quite hard to support the body on the bike; and core exercises, to strengthen the abdominal muscles and the back and which will provide a strong 'anchor' for the legs to work against.

When weight training, always start out under the guidance of a qualified instructor and take his or her advice to devise a programme of training. Start off with three sets of 12 repetitions of each exercise, using a weight that is half of the maximum you can manage. Increase weights gradually, and move up to three sets of 15 repetitions.

Always warm up thoroughly. Either cycle to the gym or try cycling on a stationary bike for at least 15 minutes. After a weight training session, do a series of stretches, and warm down, either on a stationary bike, or by cycling home.

Leg strength exercises

Strengthens: Hamstrings

Hamstring curl
Put your feet between the pads. Pull up, bend the leg until the calf muscle almost touches the back of the thigh. Release.

Leg extension

Strengthens: Quadriceps

Prepare by hooking your feet under the machine, holding on to the handles and bracing against the back. With toes pointing slightly outward, extend your lower leg until your leg is straight, then let the weight down again.

Squat

Strengthens: Quadriceps

Face forward with feet 15cm (6in) apart. Squat until your thighs are parallel with the ground. Keep your back straight. Stand up slowly, keeping your back straight. Don't lock out the knees and don't let the knees bend outward.

Leg press

Strengthens: Quadriceps

Sit with your feet 15cm (6in) apart on the plate. Push up until your legs are straight. Let the weight down until your knees are bent at about 90 degrees. Push up again. Keep the knees working in a straight line parallel with your feet.

Heel raise

Strengthens: Calf muscles

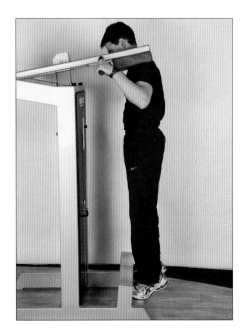

Stand with your toes on a step, with a weight across your shoulders, feet 15cm (6in) apart. Rise up until you are on tiptoes, then lower yourself down.

Crunch

Strengthens: Abdominal muscles

Lie flat on the ground with knees bent at 90 degrees. With your hands behind your head, slowly lift your shoulders off the floor. Lower the head back to the floor.

Back extension

Strengthens: Lower back

Lie on your front with the upper body hanging down. Brace feet against the supports. Slowly raise the upper body until almost straight. Lower back down.

Lat pulldown

Strengthens: Latissimus dorsi

Brace your legs under the support, reach up with straight arms and hold the bar with hands shoulder-width apart. Pull the bar down until it touches your chest. Let it back up slowly. Keep a straight back for the exercise.

Bench press

Strengthens: Pectorals, shoulders

Hold the weight and raise it with your hands above your shoulders, then push up until your arms are straightened, but don't lock them out completely. Carefully lower the weight until the bar just touches your chest.

Seated row

Strengthens: Shoulders, upper arms

Sit on a mat on the floor, with a straight back, feet braced against the footrests with knees slightly bent. Pull the bar toward the lower chest with the upper body still, until your hands touch your chest. Release slowly.

Stretches for Cyclists 1

Stretching helps loosen muscles and prevents the risk of sudden injury from working them too hard too quickly. To avoid injury and to gain the most from your workouts, you need to warm up and warm down properly.

Tight muscles can reduce power, co-ordination and endurance, all qualities that are necessary for cyclists.

To compensate for this, it is necessary to follow a regular routine of stretching, which will increase flexibility. Being more flexible will aid your recovery from workouts, and give you good posture and confidence to go with your increased energy levels and fitness.

With stretching, little and often is better than a long session once a week. By spending just 15 minutes after each training session stretching your muscles, you can make a big difference in your body's flexibility.

When performing the stretches on the next few pages, stretch until you feel the muscle tightening, relax your breathing, and hold the position for 15 seconds. Then release slowly. Don't bounce, or move too fast. Instead, gradually employ your muscles' full range of movement, and stay relaxed. Don't tense up any other muscles and don't hold your breath.

You should also be aware that stretching is not always a good idea. Never stretch when your muscles are 'cold', and listen to your body's reaction to stretching. If you feel sudden pain, stop the stretch and ensure that you have not injured yourself. Cyclists need to pay particular attention to the hamstrings and lower back. Tightness in one of these areas can lead to tightness or injury in the other. The hamstrings are not fully extended when cycling, and the repetitive nature of the cycling motion will eventually lead to your hamstrings becoming much less supple.

Stretch after your rides, but also after weight-training sessions, and any other exercises. For a little time and effort, you can gain flexibility, and prevent injury. Proper preparation is vital for anyone wanting to get fit. Going straight into a hard workout without warming up puts you at risk of injury and you will not be able to perform so well during your training session. If you finish your workout without warming down, your legs will be stiffer afterward and probably also the next day – if you have a workout planned for that day, it will not be as effective, because your muscles will be too tired to work properly.

A typical training session	
Minutes	**Activity**
15	Warm up on the bike
50	LSD ride including 30-minute tempo riding session
15	Warm down on the bike
10	Stretch
Total:	90 minutes

Warming up

To warm up, simply ride slowly, steadily increasing your workload until you can feel yourself breathing a bit more heavily. Once you get to this level, which should take about 5 minutes, maintain the same effort for another 10 minutes. Concentrate, focus and relax, especially if you have a difficult workout coming up. While your body warms itself up, your mind should be preparing itself for the workout. Warming up gets the metabolism fired up and ready to deal with the bigger effort that is going to follow. Your body temperature will rise, your heart will start to send more blood around your body and this will prepare your system for your training session.

Winding down

Once you have finished your workout, you need to put the same principle into reverse. Simply wind down by riding the last 15 minutes of your ride in a low gear, spinning your legs out at an easy speed. This allows your body to flush out some of the waste products that build up in your muscles during hard exercise. A short warm-down after every ride will reduce any leg stiffness you may have.

The advantage of cycling is that you can do your warming up and warming down on the bike – just build in about 15 minutes' worth of riding distance on to the front and back end of your ride, and the job is done.

Stretch after exercise

The best time to stretch is while your body is still warm after your workout. If this is impractical, stretch in the evening, after taking a warm shower or bath. Do as many of the stretches illustrated here as possible, paying particular attention to your legs and the lower back. If you feel you are especially inflexible or want to develop your stretching routine, speak to a physiotherapist, who will be able to advise you on specific exercises for parts of the body.

Above: Weight training and stretching will help to improve your performance on the bike by making you stronger and more flexible.

Head stretch

Stretches: Neck

Tilt head sideways to the left then the right then forward to stretch the back of the neck. Hold 5 seconds. Then tilt the head backward. Hold for 5 seconds.

Quad pull-up

Stretches: Quadriceps

Stand on one leg, and bend the other leg up behind you. Grasp the foot and pull up until you can feel the quadriceps stretching. Stretch out the other arm for balance. To increase the stretch, pull the foot up higher. Repeat with the other leg.

Gluteal stretch

Stretches: Gluteus maximus

Stand on one leg, bend it slightly, then rest your other ankle on the thigh. Bend forward until you feel the stretch in the buttock of the leg you are standing on.

Side lunge

Stretches: Inner thigh

Place feet wide apart, bend one knee so your weight goes down on it. Lower your bottom as far as you can toward the floor with your arms out straight and hands clasped for balance. Keep other leg straight. Repeat on other side.

Lateral leg stretch

Stretches: Long adductors, inner thigh

Place the feet wide apart and lean forward so your body weight rests on your hands. Widen your stance. Rotate hips inward to stretch each leg in turn.

Touching toes

Stretches: Hamstrings

With feet slightly apart and legs straight, raise arms above your head, stretch so the back lengthens, then bend down as far as you can toward your toes. Don't bend the knees. Hold for 15 seconds, breathing steadily, then stand upright.

Stretches for Cyclists 2

Specific stretches will help to improve your flexibility when you are cycling. Because the range of movement on a bike is limited – your legs don't fully extend through the pedal stroke – the muscles become stronger but tighter. These lunges and stretches aim to stretch all of the body.

Forward lunges

Stretches: Hip flexor

Put one leg in front, the other behind, and bend your front knee, keeping your back straight. Lower yourself until the knee of your back leg touches the floor.

Follow the exercise on the left: one leg in front with knee bent, and touching the floor with the other knee. For extra stretch, raise your hands as far as you can above your head.

Abdominal stretch

Stretches: Abdominal muscles

Lie on a mat on the floor, on your front with your knees, toes and chest touching the floor, and hands beside your chin.

Push up with your arms and bend the back, stretching the abdominal muscles. Keep your head level, facing forward.

Ankle rotation

Stretches: Calf muscles, shins

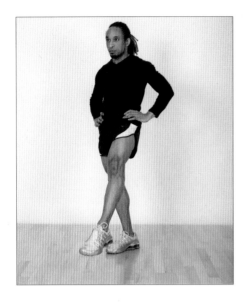

Place hands on the hips for balance. Lift left foot off the ground. Keep the other leg straight and still and rotate the left foot widely around the ankle. Change to the other side and repeat the exercise.

Calf stretch

Stretches: Calf muscles

Lean with your hands against a wall with one leg stretched out behind you and the other supporting you. Push down with the heel of your straight leg, and use your arms to get closer to the wall.

Lat stretch

Stretches: Latissimus dorsi

With hands shoulder width apart, hold a horizontal bar above your head. Let your weight suspend from the arms, to stretch the upper back and shoulders. Rest and repeat but don't overdo it.

Shoulder stretch

Stretches: Posterior shoulder

Bring one arm across your chest, just below the horizontal level. Hook the other arm around so your straight arm rests in the crook of the elbow. Use your bent arm to pull the other arm towards the body. Repeat on the other side.

Bicep stretch

Stretches: Biceps

Stretch your arm out as straight as you can behind you at shoulder height. Place your hand on a wall. Rotate your hand anticlockwise. You will feel a stretch in your biceps. Repeat the exercise using the other arm and hand.

Wrist stretch

Stretches: Forearms

Have arms straight in front of you, the palms facing outwards and the backs of the hands facing each other. Put the right hand over the left, so the palms meet, and clasp fingers. Pull hands under and towards you. Swap hands.

Cross-training for Cyclists

For racing cyclists, training on the bike and following a regime of weight training leave little time for other sports. However, taking part in other sports can help improve your overall fitness, flexibility and co-ordination.

For the keen leisure cyclist, sportive and enduro rider, playing other sports can help to improve cycling fitness and all-round fitness. Some sports can even be linked with cycling. Triathlons, which combine swimming, cycling and running, and duathlons, which involve both running and cycling, are currently enjoying a boom.

Both swimming and running are endurance sports, which means that training in these two sports will increase non-specific cardiovascular fitness, with possible benefits for cycling. These two activities also use muscle groups that cycling under-uses, which leads to greater all-round fitness and helps prevent injury.

Other sports are also good for cycling. Any team sport that involves running will boost fitness and all-round flexibility. Ball games are good for hand–eye co-ordination and balance, which will contribute to developing better bike-handling skills.

Above: Running regularly boosts endurance and offers an alternative to bike training when riding is impractical. Left: Racket sports like badminton and tennis help co-ordination and flexibility.

Swimming and running

If you have been cycling for a long time, the first thing you need to be aware of is that years of not doing any running-based sports will leave you susceptible to muscle strains, injuries and stiff legs. Before embarking on other sports, start increasing the amount of time you spend stretching.

The easiest sports for cyclists to relate to are swimming and running, which involve similar training regimes. Running uses a different set of muscles from cycling, so the important thing is to build up slowly. Buy a good pair of training shoes for running in, and for your first run, go out for a 20-minute session. Spend the first 5 minutes walking fast, then jog slowly for 10 minutes. Finally, walk for the last 5 minutes. Remember to stretch, emphasizing the legs.

The next day, go for an easy bike ride, at LSD tempo at the most. This will help your legs to recover. You may experience stiffness, especially if you ran too fast, so spin the stiffness out with some familiar cycling movement. Stretch.

Build up your running until you reach a point where you can go for a 45-minute run with no after-effects. Then you can include a couple of runs a week in your cycling training. The advantage of running is that it is much more labour-intensive than cycling – you can get the same amount of exercise in a 30-minute run as you can in 1 hour of cycling. If you are busy, running is a good way to maintain fitness for cycling.

Sports for cyclists				
Sport	**Endurance**	**Flexibility**	**Co-ordination**	**Agility**
Badminton	-	X	X	X
Cricket	-	-	X	-
Football	-	-	X	X
Martial arts	-	X	X	X
Mountaineering	X	-	-	-
Rock climbing	-	X	X	X
Rugby	-	-	X	-
Running	X	-	-	X
Swimming	X	X	-	-
Taiko drumming	-	X	X	-
Tennis	-	-	X	X
Triathlon	X	X	-	-
Ultimate Frisbee	-	X	X	X

Swimming is initially difficult for cyclists because it makes much more use of the upper body, whereas cycling emphasizes the legs. Swimming workouts also strengthen the core muscles, which will contribute to a stronger cycling style. Training for swimming also trains the mind to be more conscious of exercise economy. The more economical a cyclist is, and the more efficient his or her style, the faster they will go for the same effort. With swimming, brute strength and high fitness levels count for much less than

technique and skill. By working on the correct technique, a swimmer uses his or her fitness to maximum advantage. By applying lessons like this to cycling, you can improve cycling efficiency.

Other sports

Ball sports such as football and racket sports like tennis are also good for cyclists, offering a full physical workout. Co-ordination and agility from catching or aiming at a fast-moving object results in better reflexes and balance, and helps with bike handling and manoeuvring.

Top: Rock climbing improves balance, co-ordination and overall body strength. Above: Swimming helps to increase upper body strength and endurance.

The most important aspect of cross-training may not be the physical benefits of extra co-ordination, flexibility and endurance, but mental benefits. The training for cycling can be very serious, especially for difficult workouts. Cross-training lets cyclists enjoy sport without the pressure of performing. This can have a positive effect on mental attitude.

Keeping a Training Diary

It is important for cyclists to have long-term goals. Riding week-in, week-out can be lots of fun, but building up towards a goal is a way of getting more satisfaction and a sense of achievement out of the sport.

If you decide what you want to achieve and build up to, it is a good idea to keep a training diary. This allows you to record your progress, and to plan your workouts around your goal.

If your goal is to finish a 170km (105-mile) mountainous sportive in four months' time, and you can currently ride 100km (62 miles) before fatigue sets in, plan to increase your longest ride distance on a weekly basis until the final run-up to your event. Write your plan into your training diary, and then, as each day passes, you can write in the actual workout you did on each day. You will have a record of whether or not you are on track.

Below: Once you have a goal in mind, you can plan your training accordingly, never losing sight of the end point.

Above: All serious racing cyclists keep a training diary, to plan workouts, and to get to know their reaction to training schedules.

What to put in your training diary
Use the sample training diary opposite as a schedule for a week's training. Fill in the gaps each day. If you wish, add your own supplementary pages and end up with a record of your training activities.

At the front of the diary, insert a printout of the current year, with months across the top and days down the side. Next, write in your main goal or goals for the year. This will give you an idea of how long you have until you need to be at peak fitness, and also a good idea of how your training is going. As you cross off the days, you can compare how you are progressing with how long you have to go.

Next, print out sheets of paper similar to the diary pictured here. Each page covers one week, with space for scheduled workouts, actual workouts and all other information that you need. At the start of each week list your aims, either short- or long-term, for that week. They could include at least one long ride, two hill sessions, a fartlek session, or whatever you have planned. Your initial goal could be to ride in a build-up event for your main goal.

Take your pulse

Each day, on waking, check and write in your weight and resting pulse rate. These are good indications of your condition. A high pulse rate could indicate that you are fatigued or feeling stressed. Significant weight loss could mean that you have been training hard and need to back off for a couple of days. Once you have been up for an hour or so, give yourself a mark out of 10 for your energy level. Are you raring to go and bouncing around the house, or are you feeling flat and listless?

This score is a subjective mark, but seeing how you react physically to your training is important for gauging how hard you need to make it for further sessions. If you have two very hard weeks of training, and then take two days off, an easy day the next day and then feel 10 out of 10 on the fourth, that's a good indicator that your training has paid off. It also shows that after a hard series of workouts you feel recovered and strong by the fourth day – this information might help with peaking for your goal.

Plan ahead

For each day, write in your scheduled workout – this can be done well in advance, but it is best to leave it until you have at least started that week, so your planning can be as accurate as possible. Then, as each day passes, enter what you actually achieved. Perhaps you planned a 2-hour workout, but had to stay late at the office and only had time for an hour. Don't berate yourself for missing the training, just keep a record of what happened and see if you can compensate another day.

Lastly, at the end of the week fill in a summary of the total number of hours' training, the distance covered, your weight (including any gain or loss) and body fat percentage, if you have the means to measure it.

Over the long-term, by keeping a record of your training, you can chart your progress, and work out what training strategy will work best for you. The information gained also helps you to plan your training into the future.

Sample training diary

Date:

Aims for the week:

1 One long ride
2 Four rides total
3 Stretch every day

Monday
Weight:
Resting pulse:
Energy level:
Scheduled workout:
Actual workout:
Distance:
Time:
Intensity:

Tuesday
Weight:
Resting pulse:
Energy level:
Scheduled workout:
Actual workout:
Distance:
Time:
Intensity:

Wednesday
Weight:
Resting pulse:
Energy level:
Scheduled workout:
Actual workout:
Distance:
Time:

Thursday
Weight:
Resting pulse:
Energy level:
Scheduled workout:
Actual workout:
Distance:
Time:
Intensity:

Friday
Weight:
Resting pulse:
Energy level:
Scheduled workout:
Actual workout:
Distance:
Time:
Intensity:

Saturday
Weight:
Resting pulse:
Energy level:
Scheduled workout:
Actual workout:
Distance:
Time:
Intensity:

Sunday
Weight:
Resting pulse:
Energy level:
Scheduled workout:
Actual workout:
Distance:
Time:
Intensity:

Summary
Hours trained:
Kilometres ridden:
Weight:
Body fat percentage:

Left: It is easier to assess your fitness day by day and month by month when you fill in a training diary.

Four-week Training Schedule

All improvement through training comes from long-term planning and increasing the intensity and length of exercise. Otherwise, it is easy to just follow the same schedule week-in, week-out, which will lead to stagnation.

Racing cyclists follow the principle described earlier that fitness is like a pyramid. There is a long period of base building. Then more intense work is added before building up to a high peak of fitness. This system is known as periodization. Once your base training is done, by adding more difficult workouts, there will be a constant improvement as time goes on.

Here is a sample four-week training programme for a cyclist who has been riding for a while, but without doing specific workouts. There is a saying that you need to be fit enough to start training. It is assumed that you have been riding your bike regularly

for four to six months. If you have not, spend a little more time just working on base fitness and riding hours. Once your training schedule is about to start, write in your planned workouts in the first week of your training diary.

Week one

This first week is based entirely around long steady distance riding. The aim is to build base fitness, so week one is centred entirely around long steady distance riding (LSD). By trying too hard to go fast when you are sprinting or fast hill riding, one of two things can happen. Either you will tire yourself out and end up missing sessions, or your

Above: A recovery ride in pleasant scenery makes a change from training. Below: Long steady distance (LSD) riding is the foundation for most cycling training schedules. Long rides improve fitness and endurance.

Week one

MONDAY Rest following long ride on Sunday
TUESDAY LSD ride 1:30
WEDNESDAY Recovery ride 0:30
THURSDAY LSD ride 1:00
FRIDAY LSD ride 1:00
SATURDAY Recovery ride
SUNDAY LSD ride 2:00
TOTAL HOURS: 6:00

Week two

MONDAY Rest
TUESDAY LSD ride 1:30, including 30 minutes of spinning drills
WEDNESDAY Recovery ride 0:30
THURSDAY LSD ride 1:00
FRIDAY LSD ride 1:00, including one set of jumps
SATURDAY Rest or recovery ride
SUNDAY LSD ride 2:30
TOTAL HOURS: 6:30

Week three

MONDAY Rest
TUESDAY LSD ride 1:30, including 30 minutes of spinning drills
WEDNESDAY Recovery ride 0:30
THURSDAY LSD ride 1:30, including two sets of jumps
FRIDAY LSD ride 1:00
SATURDAY Recovery ride 0:30
SUNDAY LSD ride 2:30
TOTAL HOURS: 7:30

Week four

MONDAY Rest
TUESDAY LSD ride 1:00, including 30 minutes of spinning
WEDNESDAY Recovery ride 0:30
THURSDAY LSD ride 1:00
FRIDAY Recovery ride 0:30
SATURDAY Recovery ride 0:30
SUNDAY LSD ride 2:30
TOTAL HOURS: 6:00

fitness will initially improve, only to gradually stagnate owing to lack of a decent base.

Monday is a rest day – it usually comes after the hardest session of the week on Sunday. It is a good time to recuperate and get used to the fact the week has started. If you really feel like it, a 30-minute recovery spin would be a good opportunity to get some relaxing riding in. On Tuesday, go for an LSD ride of 1½ hours. You will be nice and fresh having taken Monday off. Wednesday is a recovery ride, then you have two days in a row of LSD training. If you wake up feeling tired on Friday, cut the session back to a recovery ride. If you are feeling great, feel free to add on 30 minutes. All through your training week you should be flexible and listen to your body. Saturday is a recovery ride, then on Sunday, the longest ride of the week – 2 hours of long steady distance.

Week two

Depending on how you reacted to week one, week two adds half an hour and incorporates some basic speed sessions, as much for the variety as for the fitness benefits. If you are tired after week one, repeat it for another one or two weeks – you need to build a solid base and progress at a realistic pace.

Monday is a rest after Sunday's long ride. On Tuesday, go for a ride of 1½ hours, and spend 30 minutes of it spinning a low gear very fast. This will build fitness and suppleness.

Wednesday is a recovery ride, and Thursday is a LSD ride. On Friday, go out for 1 hour, but test your legs out with a set of jumps. Saturday is a rest day or a recovery ride, while Sunday's distance is increased by 30 minutes.

Week three

Monday is a rest day following Sunday's long ride. Tuesday is the same as last week – a ride of 1½ hours, with 30 minutes of spinning. On Wednesday, go for a short recovery ride, followed on Thursday by a steady ride incorporating more jumps. The legs should be starting to get used to the extra effort. On Friday, if you are still feeling OK, you can do 1 hour, although you should cut this short if you are feeling tired. Saturday is a recovery ride, and then the longest ride on Sunday – 2½ hours.

Week four

During a training schedule, try to plan three weeks of improvement, then use the fourth as a consolidation week. The workouts are a bit easier, but they allow your body to rest and rebuild itself much stronger, in preparation for a new cycle

to begin the following week. Week four is similar to the other weeks in terms of ride length, though it will be beneficial to keep the spinning drills in on Tuesday. On Sunday, you'll be raring to go, so put in another long ride.

Above: Riding for around 1½ hours will build suppleness and fitness.

Eight-week Training Schedule: Intermediate

If you have successfully completed the four-week schedule you may feel ready to move on to the next stage of training. The important thing is not to move on unless you are absolutely certain you can cope and you will begin to make progress.

Once you have finished a basic four-week training schedule, assess how you feel. If you are very tired, repeat the schedule. Your body needs time to build a base, and it is more important to do that than to rush on ahead and risk overtraining. Even experienced cyclists may want to err on the side of caution and make sure that their groundwork is solid. If you feel you have improved and are ready for the next step, move on to this intermediate schedule. The emphasis will still be on a firm foundation, but with more variety, to start building upward.

Week one
Monday is a rest day following Sunday's long ride. On Tuesday start working on suppleness, but with a longer period of

Above: Professional cyclists generally follow a well-tried training schedule that has been worked out over years of experimentation and experience.

Left: When you start the eight-week training schedule, the three-hour ride on Sunday can be very hard.

spinning. On Wednesday, ride for 1 hour at a steady pace. On Thursday, the ride is 1 hour, with three or four full-on sprints. Assess how you are feeling: if you are very tired after the third sprint, don't do a fourth. Friday's ride is a recovery ride, followed by a 1-hour steady ride on Saturday, then 3 hours at a steady pace on Sunday.

Week two
It's quite a big jump this week, with the introduction of the first fartlek session, although the total hours are similar to week one. Monday is a rest after Sunday's long ride. On Tuesday, ride a

1-hour fartlek session, sprinting for signs, increasing the pace when you feel good and backing off when you are tired. Don't get carried away – some of the ride should be hard, but some of it should be at a steadier pace. On Wednesday and Thursday, steady rides will continue to build a solid foundation, with more sprints on Thursday. Friday is a recovery ride; Saturday and Sunday are steady rides, a longer one on Sunday.

Week three
The schedule is similar to week two, with a longer ride on Saturday.

Week four
After three weeks of improvement and hard work, ease off and use the fourth week to consolidate your gains. Monday

Week one

MONDAY Rest
TUESDAY LSD ride 1:00, including 30-45 minutes of spinning drills
WEDNESDAY LSD ride 1:00
THURSDAY LSD ride 1:00, including sprints
FRIDAY Recovery ride 0:30
SATURDAY LSD ride 1:00
SUNDAY LSD ride 3:00
TOTAL HOURS: 7:30

Week two

MONDAY Rest
TUESDAY Fartlek ride 1:00
WEDNESDAY LSD ride 1:00
THURSDAY LSD ride 1:00, including sprints
FRIDAY Recovery ride 0:30
SATURDAY LSD ride 1:00
SUNDAY LSD ride 3:00
TOTAL HOURS: 7:30

Week three

MONDAY Rest
TUESDAY Fartlek ride 1:00
WEDNESDAY LSD ride 1:00
THURSDAY LSD ride 1:00, including sprints
FRIDAY Recovery ride 0:30
SATURDAY LSD ride 1:30
SUNDAY LSD ride 3:00
TOTAL HOURS: 8:00

Week four

MONDAY Rest
TUESDAY LSD ride 1:00, including spinning drills
WEDNESDAY LSD ride 1:00
THURSDAY Rest
FRIDAY LSD ride 1:00
SATURDAY Recovery ride 0:30
SUNDAY LSD ride 3:00
TOTAL HOURS: 6:30

Week five

MONDAY Rest
TUESDAY Fartlek ride 1:00
WEDNESDAY LSD ride 1:30
THURSDAY LSD ride 1:00, including sprints
FRIDAY LSD ride 1:00, including 20 minutes tempo
SATURDAY Recovery ride 0:30
SUNDAY LSD ride 3:00
TOTAL HOURS: 8:00

Week six

MONDAY Rest
TUESDAY Fartlek ride 1:00
WEDNESDAY LSD ride 1:30
THURSDAY LSD ride 1:00, including sprints
FRIDAY LSD ride 1:30, including 30 minutes tempo
SATURDAY Recovery ride 0:30
SUNDAY LSD ride 3:00
TOTAL HOURS: 8:30

Week seven

MONDAY Rest
TUESDAY Fartlek ride 1:00
WEDNESDAY LSD ride 1:30
THURSDAY LSD ride 1:00, including sprints
FRIDAY LSD ride 1:30, including 30 minutes of tempo
SATURDAY Recovery ride 0:30
SUNDAY LSD ride 3:30+
TOTAL HOURS: 9:00

Week eight

MONDAY Rest
TUESDAY LSD ride 1:00, including spinning drills
WEDNESDAY LSD ride 1:00
THURSDAY Rest
FRIDAY LSD ride 1:00, including spinning drills
SATURDAY Recovery ride 0:30
SUNDAY LSD ride 3:00
TOTAL HOURS: 6:30

is a rest day, then you have two short, steady days, one with spinning drills, but no extra efforts. Thursday is a day off, then there's another steady day on Friday. After another recovery ride on Saturday, you can go for a nice long ride on Sunday, by which time you'll be ready to start working even harder.

Week five
The main improvement this week will come from the incorporation of tempo riding during Friday's ride. Sunday is a long ride, at 3 hours.

Week six
Similar to last week, but Friday's tempo session rises to 30 minutes.

Week seven
The hardest week yet, with another tempo session on Friday. Ride for longer than 3½ hours on Sunday if you feel like it.

Week eight
This is a nice easy week to round off three very hard weeks of training.

Managing your training
If your fatigue builds past manageable levels, cut back. You might have to do another four-week base-building block, or repeat a week, to get used to the extra effort without adding distance and intensity. If you get through the training, you should be in good shape.

Index

RESOURCES

Further reading
MOUNTAIN BIKING

Crowther, Nicky, *The Ultimate Mountain Bike Book* (Carlton, London, 1996)

Friel, Joe, *The Mountain Biker's Training Bible* (Velopress, Boulder, 2000)

Schmidt, Achim, *A Beginner's Guide: Mountain Biking* (Meyer and Meyer Sports Books, 2004)

Trombley, Ann, *Serious Mountain Biking* (Human Kinetics, Champaign, 2005)

Worland, Steve, *The Mountain Bike Book* (Haynes, Yeovil, 2003)

TRAINING

Bean, Anita, *The Complete Guide to Strength Training* (A & C Black, London, 2001)

Bompa, Tudor, *Periodization Training for Sports* (Human Kinetics, Champaign, 2005)

Burke, Edmund, *Serious Cycling* (Human Kinetics, Champaign, 2002)

Eberle, Suzanne, *Endurance Sports Nutrition* (Human Kinetics, Champaign, 2007)

Fiennes, Ranulph, *Fit For Life* (Little, Hethersett, 1999)

Friel, Joe, *The Cyclist's Training Bible* (Velopress, Boulder, 1997)

Janssen, Peter, *Lactate Threshold Training* (Human Kinetics, Champaign, 2001)

Kauss, David, *Mastering Your Inner Game* (Human Kinetics, Champaign, 2001)

Sleamaker, Rob, and Browning, Ray, *Serious Training for Endurance Athletes* (Human Kinetics, Champaign, 1996)

Wenzel, Kendra, and Wenzel, René, *Bike Racing 101* (Human Kinetics, Champaign, 2003)

GENERAL

Andrews, Guy, *Road Bike Maintenance* (A&C Black, London, 2008)

Ballantine, Richard, *Richard's 21st Century Bicycle Book* (Pan, London, 2000)

Franklin, John, *Cyclecraft* (The Stationery Office, 1997)

Joyce, Dan, *The CTC Guide to Family Cycling* (James Pembroke Publishing, Bath, 2008)

Roberts, Tony, *Cycling: An Introduction to the Sport* (New Holland, London, 2005)

Seaton, Matt, *On Your Bike* (Black Dog Publishing, London, 2006)

Zinn, Lennard, *Zinn and the Art of Road Bike Maintenance* (Velopress, Boulder, 2000)

SPORT

Dugard, Martin, *Chasing Lance* (Time Warner Books, London, 2005)

Fife, Graeme, *Inside the Peloton* (Mainstream, Edinburgh, 2002)

Fotheringham, William, *A Century of Cycling* (Mitchell Beazley, London, 2003)

Fotheringham, William, *Put Me Back On My Bike* (Yellow Jersey Press, London, 2002)

Wilcockson, John, *The World of Cycling* (Velopress, Boulder, 1998)

Websites

www.cyclingweekly.co.uk
www.cyclingnews.com
www.bikeradar.com
www.velonews.com

Magazines
GENERAL

Cycling Plus
Bicycling

ROAD RACING

Cycling Weekly
Cycle Sport
Procycling
Velonews
Rouleur

MOUNTAIN BIKING

MBR
Mountain Biking UK
Singletrack

CREDITS AND ACKNOWLEGEMENTS

The publisher would like to thank the following picture libraries for the use of their pictures in the book. Every effort has been made to acknowledge the pictures properly. We apologize if there are any unintentional omissions, which will be corrected in future editions.

Andy Jones: 10t, 15tl, 17t, 18b, 22, 33c, 77c, 88tr, 90 (both). Corbis: 13br, 18tr, 21tr, 31b, 32t, 35tl, 63tl, 63bl, 143br, 69tr, 69b, 75tl, 82. Fotolibra: 60, 61 (all).
Geoff Waugh: 15tr, 36, 37, 38 (both), 39 (both), 40 (both), 41 (all), 42 (both), 43 (both), 44 (all), 45 (all), 46 (both), 47 (all), 48 (both), 49 (all), 50 (both), 51 (all), 52, 53 (all), 54 (both), 55 (all), 56 (both), 57 (all), 58 (both), 59 (all), 62, 63tr, 64 (both), 65 (all), 66 (both), 67 (all). Getty: 32bl.iStockphoto: 15br, 72bl.Offside: 28, 29, 30, 31t, 34 (both), 35tr, 35b.Philip O'Connor: 8, 9, 10b, 11 (both), 12, 13tl, 13tc, 13tr, 13bl, 16t, 19t, 19c, 20t, 21tl, 22b, 23tl, 24b, 25 (all), 26 (both), 27, 33b, 70, 72t, 74 (both), 75b, 76 (both), 77tl, 77tr, 78 (both), 79 (all), 80 (all), 81 (all), 83 (all), 84 (all), 85 (all), 88bl, 89, 91, 92 (both). Photoshot: 68, 69tl. Science Photo Library: 75tr. Wheelbase: 20bl, 71.

The author and publishers thank the following individuals for their valuable contributions to this book and the companies who kindly supplied equipment and clothing for photography:
Endura
Evans Cycles
Zyro